Bus

Bus Journey Across Mexico

Exploring Mexico by Bus from California to Guatemala:
Encounters and Reflections

By

Dick Davis

Western Star Publishing LLC
P.O. Box 21511
Cheyenne, Wyoming 82003

Bus Journey across Mexico

Bus Journey Across Mexico

A Western Star Publishing LLC Book / Published by arrangement with the author

Printing History
First Printing by Western Star Publishing LLC / Dick Davis

Copyright 2010

Dick Davis

Back cover picture by Lynn Johnson

ISBN # 1-932245-06-5

Dedication:
To Toby Abrams Forst, my first excited reader, and to
Pat Buck Forbis, my last weary editor.

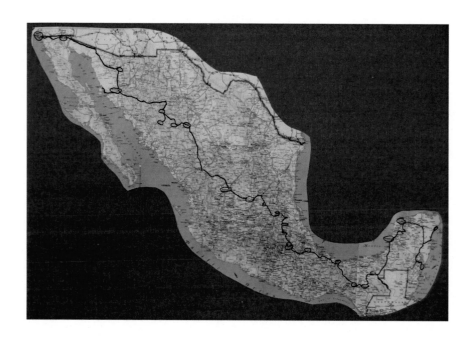

Bus Journey Across Mexico

From California to Guatemala:
Exploring Mexico's Diversity by Bus
Encounters and Reflections

Bus Journey across Mexico

Foreword

There is a phrase in Mexico, "From Tijuana to Chetumal." It means from "one extreme to the other." Tijuana touches San Diego. It's north and west and on the Pacific Ocean. Chetumal abuts Belize. It's south and east and on the Atlantic side of Mexico. Mexicans maintain, "You can get anywhere in Mexico by bus. Mexico has 800 bus companies, and they are the finest get-to-where-you're-going system in the world." The two expressions got me thinking.

Crossing Mexico by bus would be a grand adventure, and taking the bus, stopping in places I've never heard of, might make me feel like an explorer. I pulled out a large map of Mexico and looked it over. I'd avoid resorts, beaches and Mexico City. I wanted to see the heart of Mexico, the interior. I'd descend into the Copper Canyon, three times the size of the Grand Canyon, and cross deserts. I'd follow the mountainous Silver Trail, routes established by the Spanish, and seek out early missions founded by Junipero Serra. I'd stay in colonial towns. The route would take me through green jungles and past romantic waterfalls. I'd visit indigenous villages and climb Mayan pyramids. And I would put Mexico's bus system to the test.

The destination would be the journey itself. The bus would give me a feel for Mexico's topography, the roads, the travel time and the distances. I would travel with Mexicans and get a sense of culture and history.

From Tijuana to Chetumal, it's about 3000 miles, and with my meandering route it would be longer. I decided to take the trip in stages. The first stage would be from Tijuana to Zacatecas. I'd travel light and buy a shirt, sweater, socks, or whatever, along the way.

I picked up a felt-tipped pen and drew a heavy black line on my map from Tijuana to Zacatecas. For practical value, it could have been a river in the Congo. I was not familiar with the route, nor did

5

I know where I'd spend the nights. I added up the miles for this first stage on the map. There were 1600 miles of desert and mountains, with the Copper Canyon in between Tijuana and Zacatecas. There were switchback canyon roads, some gravel and dirt, and roads that were not wide enough for two cars to pass each other. I wanted to do it all by bus.

I didn't look at the bus schedules. I was told that there were buses, and they would do the job. I formed a simple plan. Start at the Tijuana bus depot, look for a bus that's headed east along the general route traced in black ink on my map, select a ride to a town, hopefully not more than four hours away, maybe six if pressed, get off, see where I had landed, stay the night, add a day if it was interesting, then repeat the process over and over again until reaching Zacatecas, or like Ambrose Bierce, I went missing.

Dick Davis

38 Days Exploring Mexico by Bus:
An Adventure from California to Guatemala

The Route: Day-by-day, town-by-town, outline:

Day   Town

1   Tijuana-Mexicali
2   Mexicali-Rio Colorado-Sonoyta-Santa Ana
3   Santa Ana-Hermosillo
4   Side Trip to Kino Bay
5   Hermosillo-Yécora-San Pedro-Creel

6   Creel Tour
7   Creel Tour
8   Creel-Batopilas
9   Batopilas Tour
10   Batopilas-Junction- Guachochi

11   Guachochi-Parral
12   Parral Tour
13   Parral-Durango- Zacatecas
14   Zacatecas-San Luis Potosí
15   San Luis Potosí- Rio Verde

16   Rio Verde-Xilitla- Mission Corridor:
          Concá, Jalpan, Landa de Matamoros, Tilco, Tancoyol
17   Xilitla-Zacualtipan
18   Zacualtipan-Pachuca
19   Pachuca-Tlaxcala
20   Tlaxcala-Puebla

21   Cordoba
22   Coatzacoalcos
23   Tuxtla Gutiérrez
24   Sumidero Canyon
25   San Cristóbal de las Casas

26	San Cristóbal de las Casa, Chamula
27	Agua Azul, Misol-Ha, Palenque
28	Yaxchilpan and Bonapak
29	Campeche
30	Campeche International Festival
31	Edzna
32	Hacienda Uayamon
33	Camino Real, Uxmal, Franciscan Missions
34	Mérida
35	Chichen Itza, Valladolid
36	Chetumal
37	Bacalar, Tulum, Playa del Carmen
38	Cancún Airport

Expenses: Transportation: buses, taxis, and vans: $605
            Hotels:………………………………...$1296
            Meals:………………………….…...$784
            Miscellaneous, fees, entrances…………$438

Total:……………………………….………..…$3133

Average cost per day:…………….………....……$82.45

Bus Journey Across Mexico: YouTube Photo Journal

Various photo journals of the journey can be viewed on YouTube, OurMexicoDickDavis. Also, you can view all photos, one by one, at dickwdavis.com.

DAY 1
Crossing the Border, the Tijuana Terminal

Bus Journey across Mexico

My friend Victor, who lives in San Diego, drove me to the U.S.-Mexican border at Tijuana. Security fences barricaded Mexico. I entered a multilevel cage, walked up and over and around and down, showed my passport, paid $21 for a tourist visa and walked through a turnstile to the largest organized army of Yellow Cabs I'd ever seen.

I was told that I could walk a couple blocks and catch a local bus to the Central Bus Terminal for $1, but I was immediately grabbed by the general of the Yellow Army, who told me that a taxi could take me to the terminal, about six miles away, for $10. I agreed so he directed me to the next available driver and off I went. At the most I was out nine bucks, but I saved time.

It was 3 p.m. when I arrived at the Tijuana Central Bus Terminal. Most of the counters were vacant. There were no lines. Clerks happily advised me about schedules and explained the differences among bus classes: Executive, First and Second.

I looked at my map, the portion that gave times and distances. I had to choose between a three-hour trip to Mexicali, or a six-hour ride to Sonoyta. Three hours seemed about right, plus I had never visited Mexicali. I chose Península Lines, Executive Class.

The experience was pure luxury. The Península Line provided a lounge, with coffee, sofa chairs, and two free computers. At 3:30 p.m. a hostess in a blue uniform called our group, and as we boarded she offered refreshments, water, beer or soda.

There were eight rows of three across seating, twenty-four seats in all, two on the left and one on the right. Each seat was ample enough for the comfort of a Sumo wrestler, and all the seats reclined.

11

There were four TVs with drop-down screens. The rear of the bus had a telephone, a bathroom and a sink. "Ironic," I thought, "bus comfort is like what the airlines used to offer, while today's air passenger is treated to the scrunched seating that once was the bus."

I asked the driver if I could sit in the first row, which was vacant. He told me to sit in my assigned seat. I learned that this was not unusual because the driver often used the first row as his storage locker. The driver was in charge, and if he wanted the curtains drawn, you wouldn't see daylight.

The driver, well-groomed, uniformed, professional, greeted us, closed the door, backed up the bus and pulled out of the terminal He followed a sign pointing to Mexicali. He plugged in a movie starring Gene Hackman and Dustin Hoffman that opened with whirlwind action and violence.

I preferred to forego the movie and watch the scenery as we drove through the desert's mountains. I peeked out between the curtains. The hillside was dotted with wrecked cars. The driver shifted into a low gear and we climbed higher into the mountains, along a cliff route. At least thirty derelict cars had gone over the side. I suspected these cars were stripped and dumped, not accidents. There were no roadside crosses.

I chatted across the aisle with Josué, a young man recently married. They lived in Mexicali but he had just started three months of training for a management position with Carl's Jr. in Tijuana. He was a graduate from a university in Ensenada and mentioned that Margarita Thompson invented the margarita at the Hotel Rivera in Ensenada. I always assumed that the name margarita, which means daisy in English, was due to the white salt on the rim of the glass that represented symbolic daisy petals.

Península Lines pulled into Mexicali a little ahead of schedule. I looked over the next day's schedules, which were posted behind the terminal's counters. There were frequent departures so there was no need to make a reservation.

I took a cab to town and asked for "la plaza central." That confused the driver and surprised me. "Which center?" my driver asked. In Mexico there is alwaya a central plaza that is surrounded by a church and the city hall. It was standard city planning. But that wasn't the case in Mexicali.

The cab driver headed for the Old Town Center. He recommended Hotel del Norte, once favored by Mexican presidents, as noted in photographs in the lobby. The last presidential visit was in 1965.

The single room rate was 485 pesos, about $45. I asked for a discount, my standard routine, but I received a pleasant "No." I checked out the room after inquiring about air conditioning.

I asked, "Does that mean refrigeration?"

"Sí, sí, hay refrigeración," she said.

In Mexico, air conditioning can mean an open window in a ventilation shaft. In my room, I put my hand up in front of the air duct. There was circulation, but I felt no cool comfort. "It's probably set at 78 degrees," I thought. If I kept asking, they'd insist it was cool. Electricity is expensive, and cool is relative.

It was still light outside so I took a walk. Next door to the hotel was a huge modern, concrete building. It looked like a first-class shopping mall. "What's that?" I asked a woman who was waiting for a red light to turn green.

"Immigration," she said. I was back at the border.

"Strange," I thought, "even when I get there, I don't know where I am."

Two blocks east I found Chapultepec Park. It was filled with tents displaying crafts and brightly painted alejibres, phantasmagorical figures from Oaxaca, which were on exhibit and for sale. I meandered around the old section and found Chinese restaurants on every block. The Chinese were among the first residents of Mexicali, which was founded in 1903. They came as farmers and more than proverbial ditch diggers; they built canals that redirected the Colorado River. The next generation went into business, became shop owners and professionals. I passed by a pagoda with a plaque stating that Nanking and Mexicali were "sister cities."

The cathedral, which was situated mid block, was the plainest Catholic Church I'd seen in a long while. It was dedicated to the Virgin of Guadalupe, Mexico's Patron Saint. With walls as barren as an underground garage, it seemed Protestant. Stained glass windows depicting disciples and saints broke the severity.

By 11 p.m. I was ready for bed, but neighbors in the adjacent room were lively. Their conversation, piped in through the ventilation duct, added to the hot air. I read for a half an hour, then put a pillow over my head and slept.

I had no real complaints. The room was adequate, not overly expensive at $45 and tastefully decorated. The shower was a power tool, like a finger massage. All the plumbing at Hotel del Norte was without water restrictors and delivered firehose pressure.

Expenses: Tourist Visa $21, hotel $45, bus $20, taxis $15, meal $7. Total: $108.

DAY 2
The End Justified the Means
Or
"All's Well That Ends Well"

Bus Journey across Mexico

It was a perfect day…the end justified the means, or I might borrow a quote, "All's Well That Ends Well."

I was up before 7 a.m. After a breakfast of huevos rancheros, coffee and fresh squeezed orange juice, I took a walk around Old Town, commonly referred to as Chinesca, which is Mexicali for Chinatown. Signs were written in Chinese and Spanish. Restaurant Mexicali Rose served Comida China (Chinese Food). There were Chinese pharmacies, restaurants, shops and herbal medicines. A China Association was founded in 1919.

I asked a man on the street, standing in front of a pharmacy, if he could tell me about the local history and the Chinese connection. He said, "Poor Cantonese immigrants sought land and opportunity in Mexico. The first Chinese came as canal builders for the Colorado River Land Company." I told the man that railroads brought Chinese laborers to California and it was interesting to hear Mexicali's parallel history.

Then with a smile he asked, "Have you heard The Legend of the Caves? It's claimed," he said, "that there were so many Chinese that they lived in underground caves and had to dig even larger caves to keep up with population growth. One day they broke their way out to the surface and appeared in Mexicali." The story sounded like the reverse of the tale told to American kids, "If you dig straight down, you'll dig a hole to China."

Then at 8:30 a.m. I turned a one-hour ride into a two-hour trip.

On my walk, I had passed the ABC Bus Company downtown. So instead of taking a taxi back to the Central Terminal, I went to ABC. That's where conversation became confused. The counter clerk was telling me they didn't have service to the Central Terminal, and I'd have to walk a few blocks to catch a city bus. At least that's what I thought. But just as I was about to follow his directions, a woman spoke up. "I'll show you where the Central is. It's only a few blocks from my stop." She told me to buy the ticket, and when she got off she would point me in the right direction. I felt confused, but this was an adventure, and I had an escort.

I bought a ticket to San Luis Rio Colorado, which I thought was the name of a neighborhood on the outer limits of Mexicali. But when the price was $3 instead of under a dollar, I should have asked more questions.

What happened was this: Because I was in the ABC station, where you caught the bus to San Luis Rio Colorado (SLRC), forty miles from Mexicali, Juana, my escort, assumed I was asking about SLRC's Central Terminal, not Mexicali's. I was on the bus when I put the puzzle together. Juana told me that ABC takes two hours instead of one due to frequent stops. I was on the "stop-and-pick-up" bus to San Luis Rio Colorado.

Juana said she came to the U.S. in 1983 and now lived in Los Angeles. She was a great-grandmother in her fifties. I asked, "What was your first job in L.A.?"

"Packed pickles in a factory." Now she baby-sits. She tried to learn English and memorized words. She said, "Grammar is difficult."

Although I took the wrong bus, I was headed in the right direction, and I was entertained. I looked over the outstretched city, stop by stop. There were vast islands of wrecked cars. "This must be auto dismantlers' heaven," I said to myself.

The bus stopped, a young college student boarded and sat in the row ahead of me. She was as slender and attractive as Audrey

18

Hepburn in *Breakfast at Tiffany's*. She had smooth, soft, mocha-colored skin, narrow lips and a fine nose. Her dark eyes were so bright they made me recall the reflections off my grandpa's black Cadillac when I'd wash and wax it in the sun. As the bus went around a curve, sunlight struck her black hair, which she must have rinsed with a reddish tint, for her hair sparkled red in the sun. She promptly opened her text to a page with a picture of B.F. Skinner. I asked, "Are you studying psychology?"

She smiled and said, "Yes," then she resumed reading. B.F. Skinner was more interesting than an old gringo, even if I might be a good subject to psychoanalyze.

We neared the end of the two-hour ride. As the bus crossed the bridge, we looked over the railing at the Rio Colorado. The river was dry. Its white sand looked more like a beach than a river. The bus turned into the city, passed small, one-story bungalows, neatly cared for, gated and fenced, painted in whites, pinks, blues and aqua greens, and adorned with red bougainvilleas.

The bus stopped on the main street. Juana picked up her shopping bag. I followed. We got off in downtown San Luis Rio Colorado, which ended the first of my three bus trips for the day.

Arriving in San Luis Rio Colorado, I thanked Juana then followed her directions to the Central, walked about six blocks and checked in at the bus station. Buses left every half hour. So far my belief that there's a convenient bus to everywhere in Mexico from everywhere in Mexico was proving to be true.

I caught the Interestales bus for Sonoyta.

The long day's ride was filled with desert views and TV videos. As we entered Sonoyta, there was a statue of President Plutarco Calles in the traffic circle where two highways met. He founded the PRI political party that governed Mexico from 1929 to 2000, until PAN's Vicente Fox broke PRI's grip and was elected president of Mexico.

General Calles defeated Pancho Villa at the battle of Agua Prieta. He was president of Mexico from 1924 to 1928 and was Mexico's strong man until his handpicked successor, Lazaro Cardenas, became president and put his own people in power.

Perhaps Calles was born or raised here. Sonoyta was not really a city. It was a linear town stretched along two intersecting highways and offered nothing attractive except for the monumental house on a hill that overlooked and overshadowed Calles' statue. The house would stand out in any setting. I asked a fellow at a taco stand, "Who owns the house that looks like a hotel on the mountain?"

He said, "That's Salcido."

"How did he get so rich?" I asked.

"Pemex, money exchange and auto parts distribution and trucking."

I had vegetable soup and a beer for lunch at The Steakhouse. Still curious, I asked the cashier about the Salcido Family. Mario Salcido was mayor of Sonoyta from 1994-1997. He built a business empire, and when he died his son inherited the family's wealth.

In an hour I had seen Sonoyta. I walked back to Bus Central. It was another three hours to Santa Ana, where I would spend the night at the Hotel Posada for $25, which included working air conditioning.

During the day, the bus followed the Ruta de las Misiones, established by Father Kino, past Caborca and Altar. Along the main street in Altar, backpacks hung from every stall and storefront like bunches of grapes ready to harvest. Altar was the staging area for young men going north. From here, it was a desert trek, and there was a history of tragedy.

A young man sat across the aisle from me on this last leg. His shoulders filled out a black T-shirt that had a cartoon character

20

figure on the front. Printed in red under the cartoon was the word "Ramcid," an American punk-rock band. We spoke and he introduced himself, Victor Tornero, a welterweight boxer on his way to his sister's wedding in Guanajuato. Victor was a friendly guy with a ready smile. He trained in Phoenix and had had twelve amateur and three professional fights, won them all, most by knockouts. He surged with joy when he spoke about knocking out an opponent.

He reminded me of Oscar de la Hoya, such a handsome, unmarked face. When we stopped, I asked if I could take his picture in front of the bus to prove, when he's famous, that we bused through Sonora Mexico together. Victor stood against the bus and clutched his fists to his chest, showing off the hammers that could strike an opponent and send him into unconsciousness.

It was dark when the bus pulled into Santa Ana. I looked for a hotel. Victor continued on his way. He'd be traveling all night.

I checked into the Hotel Posada, catty-corner from the terminal, and took a walk to shake off the ride. An Internet café was open, but I ate supper first, and while I was eating, the cybercafé closed.

I walked down the long main street. Major businesses were truck stops and motels. At a rival's hotel, with a large well-lit lobby, I saw a courtesy computer that provided email access for guests. I asked the security guard's permission to use it. He said I was welcome to check my email.

It was a long day on the bus, but because I had cut the trip into three slices, it digested well.

The hotel room was modest but clean, neat and attractive. There was a bathroom shelf for toiletries and a non-sagging mattress; nothing bends when it's on a cement slab. It was quiet and isolated, reached by a labyrinth of hallways. There was air conditioning and a reading lamp. But I never thought about the east-facing room and the thin curtain until the glare from the rising sun awakened me. From 5 to 6 a.m. I slept with the pillow over my head.

Tomorrow I'd reach Hermosillo, a major city, and the last stop before heading to the Copper Canyon, if I can get there on the bus.

Expenses: Hotel $25, meals $20, buses $34, miscellaneous $2. Total: $81.

DAY 3
Arrival in Hermosillo and a Surprise

Bus Journey across Mexico

I was Tito's first breakfast customer at 7 a.m. The restaurant looked new, and I ordered without glancing at the menu. In Mexico, if they have it, the cook will make it for you. Someone will figure out a price. I ordered, "Mexican eggs (scrambled with chili, onion, diced tomatoes), orange juice and coffee." The cook brought out a jar of Nescafé, a spoon and a mug of hot water, then returned to the kitchen. In a few minutes, I was served a hot plate of scrambled eggs, corn tortillas, French fries, crisp lettuce-carrot salad, refried beans, a pint of fresh squeezed orange juice, tortilla chips with salsa, and my coffee. My short order had gained in translation. I sampled everything, complimented the cook, "Muy rica, muy sabrosa," and paid the bill: 57 pesos ($5.25).

I bought a ticket from Santa Ana to Hermosillo for 80 pesos ($7.20), a two-hour ride.

From Tijuana to Sonoyta we followed the U.S.-Mexican border, often looking over security fences. We stopped at a number of checkpoints and even exited the bus, removed suitcases and went through a luggage inspection. I asked what they were looking for; there were no dogs sniffing for drugs and no metal detectors for weapons. A security officer told me, "Contraband merchandise that Mexicans bring home without paying taxes." This meant items purchased in the U.S. but made in China.

Thoughts on Bus Travel

Buses are comfortable and schedules convenient. You can pick a bus on this route every half hour. But you won't get peace and quiet. Standard procedure is for the driver to plug in a movie that is often prefaced by an advertisement. Then the driver sits down and turns on his own boom box. If you're up front, you may hear a mix of music and movie. The driver's music can be corrido to rap. Films are generally action and teenage, but not bad for a bus ride. Dialogue is simple, good for practicing your Spanish.

I enjoyed the drive into the neighborhoods because I was high up on a seat where I could look over houses and yards. However, most terminals have been moved away from the town centers. So after spending $7 for a two-hour ride from Santa Ana to Hermosillo, it cost me $4 for a taxi ride to get downtown.

My Theory Is Tested

I claimed and planned my trip on the assumption that, "You can get anywhere on a bus in Mexico." That proposition was tested and proven to be correct.

Thinking ahead before I left the Hermosillo's Central Bus Terminal, I asked about a bus to Creel, gateway to the Copper Canyon. I was shifted from one counter to another and was finally told to go to Los Mochis and take the train. I said, "I'd like to take Highway 16," and I showed the route on the map. Four clerks told me that there was no bus through the Sierra Madre Occidental Mountains. I was stunned. I asked, "How do people get from town to town in the mountains?" There were a number of clearly indicated towns on the map.

"Trucks, cars, donkeys," I was told in a voice that also said, "I've already told you, there are no buses."

Highway 16 connected Hermosillo to Chihuahua. So I asked, "Is there a bus to Chihuahua?" I figured that I could get off along the way and somehow get to Creel.

"Sí," the clerk said. "Take the bus to Agua Prieta and from Agua Prieta to Chihuahua." I was dumbfounded. That's like going from San Francisco to Los Angeles via Reno, Nevada. I began to wonder just how isolated was the Copper Canyon and if my plan was viable. I left the terminal with a numb mind.

Across the street I saw a small office for another bus line. Hmmm, maybe, "No" might mean "Not from our terminal on our buses," or maybe they just hadn't had anyone inquire before. Going into the Sierra Madre is not your standard trip. Just ask Humphrey Bogart.

I crossed the street and inquired. A woman, who was eager to help, told me that on Monday through Friday mornings Transportes Chaves picked up passengers at 6:30 a.m. at the TBC Station and left for Yecora, which on the map was about halfway to Creel.

"Are there buses in the Sierra?" I asked.

"Yes," she assured me.

I was back in business, if only halfway. There had to be a connection to the second half. I'd find out when I arrived in Yecora.

Monday, 6:30 a.m. at the TBC Terminal, I would catch the Transportes Chaves bus, but I had a weekend to spend in Hermosillo.

I settled into Hotel San Andres. I needed a walk after the morning bus ride and headed downtown, just trying to get a sense of the general area and where my hotel was located.

Green spots and trees in the distance indicated parks. I found the university then took a left on a main street, passed VIPS Restaurant and signs indicating directions to the cathedral, museum and the Casa Cultura.

Kino Hotel, a block off the main street, intrigued me with its architecture, if not colonial, 19th century classic. I asked to see a room and took a tour of the hotel. It had been remodeled many times over the years. The rooms were attractive and had refrigerators and microwaves for about $50 a night.

To the left of the main lobby there was a museum and a history of the hotel. Antique phonographs, telephones, typewriters, and an electric fan, all in working order, were on display. A card labeled each item, noting the manufacturer and the year. The oldest phonograph, an 1896 Edison cylinder model, looked new. There was a range of models from 1896 to 1924. A platter replaced the cylinder. The changes seemed so slow, 28 years, still mechanical, with a big horn sticking out like you see in the *His Master's Voice* trademark. There were telephones with cranks, both wall and tabletop models. The 1936 Remington typewriter looked like the one I hammered on in college. I thought of the rapid changes we've had since the computer-Internet age. I couldn't envision a computer product that would be the same after three decades.

Then, I found myself at the edge of an inner courtyard. I stopped. It appeared there was a private party. I learned that it was more than a fiesta.

In Mexico, the Quinceañera (celebration of a girl's 15th birthday) is similar to a Debutante Ball, but not necessarily an upper-class event. It's viewed as one of the greatest moments of a young lady's life, and one of the happiest. Weddings are milestones too, but some are regretted, a Quinceañera, never.

Families sacrifice for the celebration. Often, parents, like soccer moms, or Little League dads, live the joy through their children.

I had never been to a Quinceañera before that day in Hermosillo.

When I walked into the courtyard of the Kino Hotel, tables, chairs, music and refreshments were set up. There were fifteen maids of honor, all wearing apricot-colored ballroom gowns. I hesitated. It looked like a private party. A lady came over to welcome me, thinking that I was a guest. "No, I'm just a tourist," I said, "but is this a wedding party?" The lady laughed and told me that it was a retirement party for Guadalupe Lopez, who had worked for the Kino Hotel for twenty-four years.

A young man, who introduced himself as Juan Carlos Jimenez, joined us. He was in charge of the hotel's tourist packages. He invited me to join the celebration. He led me to a circle of chairs, introduced me to friends, brought a Coke, and we chatted.

Two piñatas hung from the patio's rafters, a five-foot tall Tecate Beer Can, and an equally large Gran Dama (Great Lady), both made of papier-mâché. The maids of honor formed a line.

Juan Carlos explained, "Guadalupe never had a Quinceañera; her family could not afford it, so her friends on the hotel staff decided to make her retirement party her Quinceañera."

Music began. It was the *Triumphal March* from Aida. Armando Bernard Noriega, owner of the hotel, gave his arm to Guadalupe, who was dressed in white, and led her in procession followed by her damas de honor. They circled the center fountain followed by the train of ladies. Men got up from their chairs to offer an arm to each lady and joined in the procession. Smiles and joy and laughter filled the courtyard. When the procession stopped, Sr. Armando Bernard danced the first waltz with Guadalupe. One by one men cut in to dance with her.

Guadalupe moved cross-court in front of a cake that was decorated in color with Cinderella. Guadalupe stood for photos. I greeted her, spoke about her retirement and her plans, and thanked her for being her guest at her Quinceañera. I couldn't imagine a

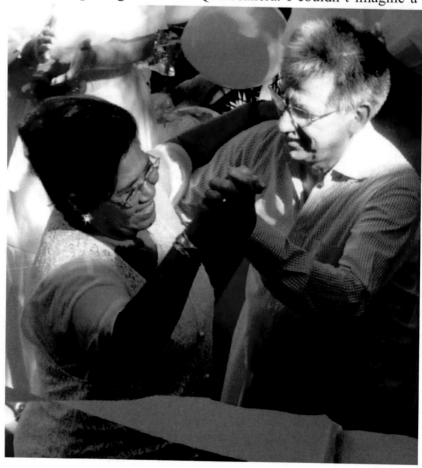

more successful Quinceañera or one with more respect and love for the celebrant.

Downtown Hermosillo was quiet. I walked past the museum to a central park with a statue of Jesús García. I knew his name from a corrido, the song *Máquina 501* (*Locomotive 501*). In 1907, Nacozari, a mining town in Sonora, was threatened with destruction when a dynamite-laden train caught fire. Alone, Jesús took over Locomotive 501 and drove the burning train to the edge of town. He needed only a few more yards to reach safety himself when the dynamite exploded. Jesús lost his life, but saved the town and hundreds of lives. In his honor, the town was renamed, Nacozari de García.

I caught a taxi to the top of Cerro Campana (Bell-shaped Hill) that overlooked Hermosillo. The view is like looking over Phoenix from Pinnacle Peak.

The taxi took me back to my hotel. I rushed a meal and changed into my only long-sleeved shirt. I had seen a poster advertising *La Lágrima* (*The Tear*). The Ballet Company at the Casa Cultura would perform the dance at 8 p.m.

It was a young, college-aged crowd. I purchased a single, general-admission ticket for 60 pesos ($5.50). I read the program and tried to understand the story. The best I could get from it was a quote from the director, Adriana Castaños, "Dance is a social act."

The performance and my interpretation: Five dancers appeared and the dance was choreographed in five stages. In the twilight of light and shadow, the first scene opened with two dancers, nude except for briefs. The male-and-female couple maintained a pose while a piano played in the background. They appeared to be Adam and Eve, or perhaps Lucy and Neanderthal, and as the danced progress I opted for the Darwinian interpretation.

The dance, like the music, began simply. One dance flowed into another and became more intricate. In part two, three male comic dancers replaced Adam and Eve. They appeared to be squirrels.

The point seemed to be that dancers imitated the animal kingdom. The nudity gave way to moderate dress.

In the next set, two females and three males discover each other. It appeared to be love, romance and boy meets girl. Both the dance and the music developed. The music and score became more complex. As instruments were added, a full orchestra was heard.

The theme of birth and children appeared. In the climax, the dancers were clothed as if costumed for a Mardi Gras. There was an illusion to *Cats* and most impressively, the dance and music, fully developed, concluded with a stylized interpretation of the *Mexican Hat Dance*.

Dance, music, clothes, romance evolved and the rhythm of the *Mexican Hat Dance*, with its staccato footwork, brought us back to the origin of dance, the animal kingdom. Dance had developed and progressed in a "social act."

Expenses: Hotel $35, bus $7.50, meals $15, taxis $19, dance $5.50. Total: $82.

DAY 4
Sea of Cortez: Kino Bay College Heaven

Bus Journey across Mexico

My sister-in-law once spent a college vacation at the beach on Kino Bay in the Sea of Cortez, about a two-hour drive from Hermosillo. Because she wondered if it had changed, I asked my friend Bernardo if he could ask his friends in Hermosillo if I could spend a Sunday with them at the beach.

Bernardo's friends, Christian and Etty, became my hosts for the day. This was the last day of spring vacation, and their son had been spending the week with college friends at Kino Bay. I could visit the Sea of Cortez, and Christian and Etty could pick up their son.

Kino Bay was packed with college students. Ten kilometers of beach homes lined Kino Bay along the one-road access. Traffic was heavy. All I saw were bumpers and bikinis for six miles. We drove to an overlook that gave us an excellent view of the Sea of Cortez, the beach, the Sierras and the desert in colorful palettes of blues, tans and browns.

We walked along the beach. Young men were playing soccer, with beer cans for a goal. A yellow, red and blue umbrella stood out in contrast to the sun-sparkling beach. The white seashells, kicked up by waves and tide, formed a crunchy path along the Sea of Cortez.

I felt like I needed a pass to enter because I was the oldest guy on Kino Beach. We were told that the college crowd was a once-a-year phenomenon. For the rest of the year, fishing and tranquility would reign.

We lunched at Mariscos Judy, a beach, seafood restaurant. Judy, an American, married a Mayan chef, and they opened this restaurant. We ordered the specialty, a combination plate of shrimp, fried fish, manta ray, vegetables, salad and cold beer. I mentioned my sister-in-law's fond memory and we ordered a second beer.

Expenses: Hotel $35, breakfast $6, miscellaneous $4. Total: $45.

DAY 5
Up Before the Rooster, The Road to Creel

Bus Journey across Mexico

I left the Hermosillo Bus Terminal feeling that my trip might be altered. I was nearly convinced that I'd be going south to Los Mochis and would have to catch the Copper Canyon train to Creel.

My belief that you can get anywhere in Mexico on a bus had been reconfirmed when the clerk at TBC, a small terminal, separate from the Central, told me to take the Transportes Chaves bus to Yecora and that there would be connecting buses in the Sierras. Yet I had doubts.

Transportes Chaves was ready at 6:30 a.m. in Hermosillo and left shortly after 7 a.m. It was Second Class, which in this case meant very comfortable sofa-like seats. The bus seated forty passengers, without a TV or onboard bathroom. Executive Class would be luxury with super-wide seats, twenty-four passengers, TV, and bathroom. First Class was thirty-two seats, with TV and a bathroom. The bathroom removes eight seats that you find on

Second Class. Third Class is generally a shorter bus; windows open for fresh air. It looks like a school bus.

I preferred the Second Class without the TV and curtains. In First Class I felt like I was in a rolling movie theater and missing the view.

The bus headed east across the plains, looking directly at the Sierra Madre Occidental, brown and barren. The tall, jagged-edged peaks looked like a saw, which the word *sierra* means. We climbed the low hills then entered the Sierras where twists and turns slowed our progress. It was a 180-mile, five-and-one-half-hour trip. It became six hours when we stopped for a lunch break near Yecora, just before our descent through a majestic, wind-eroded canyon, where the driver pointed out various forms. There were craggy faces, mushrooms and turtles.

We drove past Tepoca, a town with glittering galvanized roofs in the sun. I asked Jesús Ramon, my seatmate, "What's the industry here?"

I expected, "Sawmill, lumber, maybe mining." But Jesús said, "Marijuana." I let that drop.

Just before 2 p.m., we arrived in Yecora, a dusty and wind-swept town of about a thousand residents. It was obvious that the best place to eat was our stop before reaching the town. Yecora reminded me of the Texas town in *The Last Picture Show*, a place you wanted to be from, not going to. The Pemex gas station was the highlight. I quickly became concerned that I'd be spending a night here. Three young men stood across from the Pemex on the highway. I asked it they were waiting for a ride or if there was a bus.

The tallest fellow, who looked like a student, said there would be an Estrella Blanca (White Star) bus within a few minutes. It was the Obregon-to-Chihuahua bus that could take me most of the way to Creel. What good fortune!

Within fifteen minutes I flagged down the bus. As I went to board the Estrella Blanca bus, the driver told me, "There are no seats."

I said, "That's okay; I can stand."

The driver said he could take me as far as San Pedro, a seven-hour ride, and then I could connect to Creel.

No seat was the best seat. I stood on the steps in the door well. Standing in the bus's entrance steps, I had an expansive view. I got off and on at least ten times as we stopped and dropped off passengers and picked up new ones. Seats were always full, and I maintained my windshield panorama station. I had a better view than the driver because I did not have to watch the road.

It was a long day and a lonely road. I don't think I saw five vehicles all day, but with the changes and connections, I hardly noticed the time. The Sierras were magnificent, with pipe-organ and saguaro cacti in bloom, encinos (scrub oaks), long-needle pines, cypress pines and the incredible flora that changed with the elevation, like Sedona, Arizona.

A coyote ran across the road, stopped and turned to watch us pass. Squirrels frequently raced across the road, darted into the brush or found a safe crevice among the rocks. One squirrel, munching a dead snake on the highway, was so deaf, or concentrating on his meal, that it didn't even flinch as the bus roared by.

The Estrella Blanca halted at a rest stop. We were given twenty minutes. I took a short walk and was standing on the highway, making sure I wasn't left behind, when I saw a hiker dressed in green fatigues coming down the hill towards me. He had a walking stick and a backpack. As he neared, I greeted him in Spanish. He explained why he was there. "I'm mapping the area using GPS for a Canadian company. We're mapping minerals." He told me he'd be there for three weeks.

The bus driver waved me over to board. I told the hiker, "Goodbye and good luck."

The bus slowed down in the mountains, and it was great to travel with the driver and co-driver. They told stories and joked with the passengers. Because the trip took fourteen hours from Obregon to Chihuahua, the drivers switched off.

From time to time the driver played a Mexican-music CD. Selena was his favorite singer. I asked for José Alfredo Jiménez, and we listened to *José's Exitos* (*Greatest Hits*). Because Estrella Blanca was Second Class, the driver's music did not compete with a TV.

The bus dropped me at San Pedro, a crossroads, at 9 p.m. I stepped out of the bus and into a night blacker than a coalmine. Where was the horizon? I couldn't tell were the Earth left off and the sky began. I looked up and there it was, the Milky Way, spread out like a bride's train, which I hadn't seen for years.

Two log cabins were San Pedro. One was a restaurant with no bathroom, or at least for men it was the behind the building in the shadows. The other cabin seemed to be a house. I could see a weak, yellow light from within.

My heart raced as my thoughts warned, "What if there is no bus?" I'm too old for an overnight in a field with cows. I waited. Shadows approached. A family of four crossed the road and assured me that the Noreste bus would arrive shortly.

We waited about half an hour. There were cheers when the Noreste bus pulled off the highway, rounded the corner and stopped. There were plenty of seats for the one-and-one-half-hour ride to Creel. I was surprised. I never thought I'd arrive in Creel my first night out from Hermosillo.

The Noreste bus was First Class, with TV but no bathroom. So I was confused as to whose definition was reliable. Maybe different companies have different rankings. I was ready to sit and watch a film after standing for seven hours. The movie was *Aviator*, the story of Howard Hughes. The film was in English without subtitles. I think I was the only one on the bus who understood the dialogue.

In Creel, Victor, a guide, met the bus. He was eager to show me a hotel. At 11 p.m. I was eager, too. He gave me a pitch on tours as we walked two blocks to a hotel. It had no name but was recently remodeled, and the price was $25, a bargain.

I asked for a restaurant; Victor took me to Veronica. I asked what I owed him. He said, "Nothing." He was hoping that I'd come by in the morning and look over the tours. I thanked him, but also gave him 20 pesos for his advice and help.

I entered Veronica's at the same time as another man. We were the last customers. I ordered vegetable soup that was mostly cauiflower, and a beer. I greeted the other man, who seated himself across from my table. He carried a carbine rifle, wore green camouflage fatigues with a U.S. flag patch, and some army insignia on his shoulder. He said that he was a "policía" in Urique and he invited me to sit at his table.

I asked about his rifle. He showed me his ID card, Leonardo Lopez Carrillo. He unfolded an official document, which was his permit to carry a .223 carbine. He was the strangest looking cop I ever saw, but the papers were all documented, stamped and notarized. I asked if I could snap his picture. He stood in front the fireplace. I felt like I was taking the picture of the last man who rode with Pancho Villa.

Expenses: Buses $40, meals $14, hotel $25, miscellaneous $2. Total: $81.

DAY 6
Creel: Eco-tourist's Delight

Bus Journey across Mexico

I spent the morning trying to catch up on email. When you're in Creel, the connection is slow, and the computer surely set the world record for "Error Page."

I checked out the tours. All sounded like they would take the visitor to an eco-tourist paradise. They added a visit to the Tarahumaras, who call themselves the Raramuri (Light Feet). They are respected for long-distance running and have been known to stalk and chase deer to the point of the animal's exhaustion. Most Tarahumara are nomadic, often living in natural cave shelters. Religious beliefs are a syncretic melding of Catholic Christianity with indigenous customs. One could join a tour group or go alone with a map: bike, motorbike, rent-a-car or hike. The tourist center offered free maps for the hiker, camper and overnighter. I wondered if Leonardo Lopez Carrillo protected the popular hiking route from Creel to Urique.

I took the tour that was advertised at 120 pesos. The price assumed a minimum of six tourists. We were only three, so the

price was adjusted to 200 pesos ($19) each, which was fair.

Martin was our driver. I rode shotgun. The couple behind was from Norway, or at least Einar was Norwegian. His girlfriend Carmen

47

was Mexican from Monterrey. She had earned a scholarship and was studying in Norway for her Master's. She said, "I love the four seasons and winters in Norway!" They spoke English and Norwegian. This was Einar's first trip to Mexico; he was lost in Spanish.

Tour Number 1 took us to Arareco Lake and Cascada Cusarare, where we walked, hiked and took photographs. A herd of goats came by the pine trees. They were watched over by Tarahumara women, who were dressed in yellows and reds with scarves on their heads. We admired the lake but Cusarare Falls were a dribble. Martin said they were in the seventh year of a drought, and the famous Basaseachi Falls, higher than Yosemite Falls, were completely dry.

We visited the restored San Miguel Mission and museum, with its outstanding oil paintings of saints from the 18th century. I entered the church, now plain and barren. All paintings had been removed for their protection and placed in the museum. The walls were whitewashed and the windows accented with a broad band painted brick red.

Four women sat silently in the church against the right wall on benches, the only seats in the church. In the center of the sanctuary in front of the altar there was a small flower-adorned cardboard casket. The women were silently grieving for a child.

We made our last stop at the home of a Tarahumara family. They opened their home to tourists for a monetary gratuity. It was a cave under an overhanging rock. The front of it was walled up with stones, leaving space for a door. Dark smoke billowed from a stovepipe chimney. Soot stained the rock-cliff face. Inside, there was a kitchen, cupboards, two beds, chairs, a table and a small hammock, which was used as a cradle. Water was hand carried in buckets from a nearby well. It was smoky; my photos looked like I took them in a fog.

The daughter told me that her father died in a rockslide accident while building a highway. The widow was tenderly rocking an infant in the hammock cradle. The daughter was dressed in a casual black sleeveless top and jeans, rather than the bright colors generally preferred by the indigenous. She lived in town and worked at a hotel. She was a single mother of two and earned $10 a day. She said she was born in the cave. The children lived here with her mother. She had a primary school education and left home at age fourteen to work.

I walked to the edge of town to get a panoramic view. Creel was a rustic town. Log buildings gave it a western feel. It was located in a valley and was surrounded by forests. There were Ponderosa pines, long-needled pines, short-needled pines and Triste (Sad) pines, whose needles drooped as if weeping. Sculptured rock formations framed Creel to the east. To the west, on the hill overlooking Creel, there was a giant white Cristo Rey (Statue of Christ).

Expenses: Hotel $25, meals $19, tour $20, Internet $2. Total: $66.

DAY 7
Creel: The Flying Stone

Bus Journey across Mexico

The Norwegian-Mexican couple enjoyed hearing about my Mexican experiences and asked if we could join up together. We signed up for Tour Number 2 the next day as a threesome and for the bus to Batopilas in the heart of the Copper Canyon.

Carmen's Master's thesis was on eco-tourism and my comments about the places I'd been fit her theme. She'd studied photography

for three years in Paris and said she'd like to video my remarks.

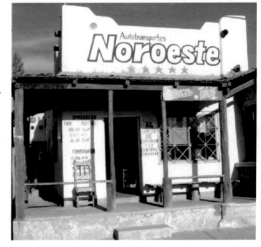

At 7 a.m. I was up and walking the streets of Creel in the cold, fresh morning air. I walked to the edge of town, past the train station and the Noreste bus depot. I walked over a bridge; the riverbed below was rock, dry sand and weeds.

A fellow was leaning against the bridge. I asked,

"When does it rain?"

"June and July," he said.

"And snow?"

"December," he said.

"How much snow do you get? I asked.

He took his hands, palms facing each other, and showed me a measure of about seven inches. "This is a little he said. Then he moved his hands apart to about ten inches. "This is a little more," and parting his palms to about a foot he said, "This is a lot."

I walked back to town. In this isolated place, there was a Banco Santander with an ATM. In the main street, drivers talked on their cell phones. You could sit down to a treat at the Holanda Ice Cream Parlor or choose among dozens of restaurants. It was hard to believe that the hotels would ever fill up, there were so many. But I was told that during Easter and Christmas it was wise to have a reservation.

There were nearly as many Tarahumara craft and gift shops as restaurants. The Tarahumaras brought their crafts to the plaza to sell, and they worked there creating new ones.

Tour #2: Highlight Piedra Volador

Wednesday I met Einar and Carmen for the tour that took us to Divisadero, Piedra Volador, Piedra Fertilidad and Elephant Rock. The rock formations were impressive, but the canyon, with its sheer vertical drops, weakened my knees. The highlight was the Piedra Volador (Flying Stone), which is actually a large stone that wobbles when someone walks on it. The granite stone was the size of a farm tractor tire. It was perched at the end of a rock abutment jutting out into the canyon, which was about twenty feet wide then narrowed as you walked towards the cliff. The Balancing Rock was egg-shaped stone and rested on top of a flat rock.

Our driver, Salvador, walked out on the jutting abutment, hopped on the egg-shaped stone and then shifted his weight. The stone rocked back and forth. It was a Flying Stone. We were invited to follow his example, but we declined. That pleased Salvador as he felt pride in his courage.

Salvador drove us back to Divisadero where one of the first Copper Canyon hotels was built. We shopped and ate lunch. Today had been a great tour, although it was a heart stopper for me.

I walked back to my hotel. A building was painted with murals depicting the Tarahumara. One mural caught my attention. It was plain, just a woman, wearing a white blouse. She was seated, with her hands resting on her red polka-dotted skirt, a headband around her hair. Her thoughts were written on the wall:

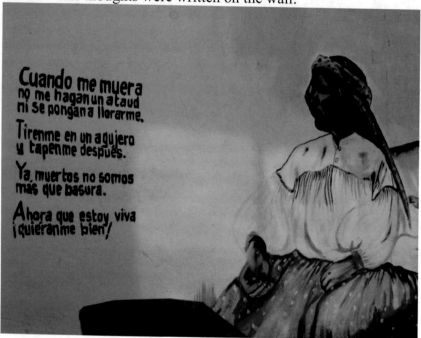

Cuando me muera
No me hagan un ataud
Ni se pongan a llorarme.

Tirenme en un agujero
Y tapenme despues.
Ya muertos no somos
Más que basura.

Ahora que estoy viva
Quiéranme bien.

When I die
Do not make me a coffin
Or start to cry.

Throw me in a hole
And cover me over.
When we die we are no
More than trash.

While I'm living
Love me completely.

Expenses: Hotel $25, meals $16, tours $15, bus $16 miscellaneous $7. Total: $79.

DAY 8
The Road to Batopilas, Arrival at the Bottom of Copper Canyon

Bus Journey across Mexico

I woke before the roosters crowed because my sleep was broken multiple times throughout the night by barking dogs. I left my modest hotel and arrived before Carmen and Einar at Hotel Margarita, a beautiful western-rustic lodge, which had the only restaurant open for breakfast at 7 a.m. I had time to appreciate the brilliantly colored murals, scenes depicting Tarahumara dances and tribal life, which decorated the dining room walls.

We toured the sites outside Creel the day before. Today we were headed deep into Copper Canyon. We caught the Transportes Turisticos de la Alta y Baja bus on the main street. Transportes ran a daily service for 170 pesos ($15), but the schedule varied.

It was a short bus, twenty-four seats, ideal for the mountain's sharp curves and switchbacks. There were fifteen passengers. I sat in the rear and faced forward. An American priest, Father Dominic, whose parish was Batopilas, was reading the Bible. A Mexican construction worker was reading Shakespeare's *"Othello"* in Spanish. "What are the odds?" I wondered.

I asked Father Dominic, "What's the weather likely to be in Batopilas?"

He said, "We have two seasons: hot and dry, and hot and humid. The rainy season is June and July."

It's a lonely road from Creel to Batopilas, a 5800-foot descent from Creel to the bottom of Copper Canyon, three times the size of the Grand Canyon. It is home to 60,000 Tarahumara (Raramuri people) and a trip back in time to the 19th century where treasure in gold and silver was gouged from Mother Earth. The few trucks and worn-out cars on the road were filled with passengers. A hitchhiker would rarely find a lift.

The paved road from Creel to the junction was 75 km (47 miles). Then the bus turned west onto a dirt road for 65 km (37 miles) to Batopilas. Travel time was five hours. If the entire road were paved and flat, I could bike the route in less time.

At the junction, our driver shifted into low and ground the gears. We were in a pine forest following a ridge. The road was cliffhanger narrow, made of twists and mountain switchbacks. Then a canyon, one of seven, came into view. Majestic cliffs rose like guardians painted in multicolored red, white, brown layers and streaked with green. Here was nature's chronology of time. Sedimentary stone, slate, rockslides, volcanic lava flows, white tufa and igneous rock were present.

I didn't notice the bus swerve, but our driver did. He stopped and checked the tires. He got down and on his belly crawled under the rear axle, poked a tire with a wrench handle and said, "The inside tire is flat." He squiggled back out from under the bus, dusty as if a baker had powdered him. He set the brake, placed a rock under the front tire and went to release the spare tire that looked like a donut hanging under the bus. He loosened the lug nuts then jacked up the bus. The change was quick, and it gave us a moment to see the canyon, stretch and talk.

Back on the bus, we passed by old mines, peered down at the river and crossed an iron trestle bridge that was supported by mammoth stone piers. We were coming into Batopilas. As we crossed the bridge we could see cows along the riverbank and Tarahumara women washing their clothes in the river.

Batopilas was a linear town forced to stretch two miles along the river because steep canyon walls hemmed it in. We drove down the narrow road toward the center. We encountered a truck that backed up and pulled over to let us pass. A minor increase in the number of vehicles would be a major problem for Batopilas.

We drove past a long, well-kept colonial-style building with a blue-tiled cupola. It was a private chapel and part of the luxury by-reservation-only Hotel Riverside. There was no name on the building. The bus made its final turn, and the splendid sight of the town square greeted us, with an ironwork bandstand framed in the background by a brightly colored mural of Tarahumara children.

Children played in the street. There was a soccer game, and a boy and his sister bounced on a tire trying to make one another lose balance. Cows roamed freely, seemed to own the street, paid us little attention and were the town's street sweepers, licking up fallen leaves that lay on the cobblestones. I saw more cows in Batopilas than I've ever seen in Texas.

Othello (the nickname for the man reading Shakespeare) suggested Mary's Hotel. Several of us entered and asked to see a room. Because the owner was out, the maid offered to show us a room.

The office was locked; the maid tried to jimmy the latch with a table knife. I said, "Pardon me. My misspent youth might be handy here." I took the knife and popped the lock open. There was mild surprise from onlookers.

61

Mary's did not have room for all of us. I noted there was no air-conditioning. At the end of the plaza was Juanita's. It was attractive, with an inner patio, overlooked the river and offered central air-conditioning. Juanita charged $20 a night for a single.

I took a walk before dinner. There was a library and an Internet at the Centro Comunitario de Aprendizaje I retraced the main street back to the green iron bridge. Near the bridge was an artist's studio. Luis was a German artist who chose Batopilas for his home and studio. I looked at the fine detailed paintings. "Are they pen and ink?" I asked.

"No, they are watercolors."

I had promised to meet Carmen and Einar for dinner so I started to walk back. I passed a shack that was selling beer and soft drinks. A man spoke up. He looked like a wrangler. He wore a cowboy hat and white cowboy shirt. He was solid, with muscular arms and a mustache.

"Are you with a group?" he asked.

"No, I'm by myself," I said.

He introduced himself, "Arturo, guide."

We talked and agreed to meet at 8:30 a.m. for a comprehensive tour of Satevo, Mission San Miguel Archangel, Eagle's Nest, the Tarahumara Village and San Miguel Mine. I hoped that Carmen and Einar would join me and share the expense.

Expenses: Hotel Juanita $20, meals $18. Total: $38.

DAY 9
The Mission, the Mine and Dancing

Bus Journey across Mexico

Carmen and Einar were enthusiastic and agreed to join Arturo's Tour and split the cost.

They were staying at Hotel Casa Real with a squad of motorcyclists: business and professional men who could afford the bikes and enjoyed the challenge of the canyon's steep unpaved roads. One biker, Mike Madden, from San Francisco Bay Area, near my home, said, "I graduated from a school you never heard of, the Maritime Academy."

I fished in my brain and came up with, "Do you know Tom Stapleton?"

"Yes, where is Tom?" Six Degrees of Separation turned out to be only one.

The next morning, Arturo showed up at 8:30 a.m. with his tour-mobile, a pickup truck outfitted with automobile bench seats in the truck bed. He surprised us with two additions, Heidi and Amber, mother and daughter, whom we had seen on the bus ride into the canyon. Arturo said we could split the cost five ways. I was surprised by his generosity. A four-hour tour, $30 divided by five, brought the price down to $6 each.

I hopped in the back. Arturo drove a block, stopped at a store and called out for gas. There were no gas stations in Batopilas. A woman, wearing a pink tank top and jeans with a red stripe highlighting the pant's seam came out from the store with a four-gallon white plastic container. She inserted a rubber tube into the gas container. The woman sucked on the tube and siphoned the gas from the plastic container into the truck's tank.

We drove out of Batopilas towards Satevo, the site of an early Spanish mission church. We bounced and weaved on the rough road. I told Carmen, "I haven't had such a great ride since my dad hauled trash and I got to ride in back, but without this comfort."

We had a great view of the canyon, the steep walls, the river, the desert cacti in bloom and the cows. "More cows than Texas," I said. A bull faced off the truck then changed his mind.

Arturo stopped when Mission San Miguel Archangel came into view. It was a *National Geographic* picture-perfect view: a canyon, river, swinging bridge, ancient bell-towered mission, originally built in 1707, set in a valley with a mountain backdrop.

There was a small community living in Satevo. Arturo asked a girl to get the key to the San Miguel Archangel church. The interior was simple, without benches. The building was unusual. It was built of red bricks and designed in the form of a Roman cross, the cross arms rounded, not squared off.

Outside I learned about the *pitalla* tree, a hands-on experience. It looked like a young cottonwood. When I stepped up on a stone wall for a better angle to photograph San Miguel Archangel, I put my hand on the *pitalla* tree for support. My hand jumped in reflex. It was my first opportunity ever to use the tweezers in my Swiss Army knife. Seven needles implanted themselves into my left hand. The four in my fingers I pulled out with my right hand. But three broke off in my palm, and once again I praised the Swiss.

The girl who brought the key also came with a guitar. Arturo asked the girl about her progress and what she could play as he tuned the guitar. She was shy but played for us. Arturo asked for songs. I suggested any song by José Alfredo Jiménez. Arturo played *Camino de Guanajuato*. He encouraged me to sing along. I knew some of the verses but needed Arturo to prompt me. We sang, "No vale nada la vida…" (Life is worth nothing). The song is a miner's lament.

Arturo shifted to a waltz. Here we were at the bottom of the Copper Canyon, and Arturo's strumming the guitar. There was a smooth surface, part of the old church courtyard, near the low stonewalls where Arturo sat and played. I asked Heidi, "Would you care to dance?" We danced; everyone laughed.

Amber picked up the guitar. She sang blues. Here in the desert, she entertained us with "Give Me a Reason." She sang slowly, beautifully, as if touched by Billy Holliday.

I didn't see the Tarahumara village on the hill among the cacti and the brush until Arturo pointed it out. We followed Arturo up the path and as we neared the village, walking up the knoll, we saw trash strewn everywhere. There were scraps of plastic snagged on cacti, a pink child's cap, embroidered with a smiling Mickey

67

Mouse, a discarded red sweater, plastic soda bottles and aluminum cans.

It really wasn't a village but a small family community. Only women and children were present. Arturo said we could talk, visit and take pictures. A gift was expected.

We received a mixed reception. We met bright smiles and easy conversation. Then again, there were blank stares that I felt were either resentful or hostile. I asked Arturo. He said, "No, you are welcomed, but some are just shy."

I asked one of the young ladies, "Do you live here year around?"

"No," she said, "we move higher up during the rainy season."

The Tarahumara women were dressed in bright colors, broad skirts, and billowy blouses. They have an aesthetic sense of color. I said, "They are the canyon's desert flowers, so brightly colorful." The homes were primitive. There were wood-burning stoves, improvised, made of metal castoffs and a stone *metate* for grinding corn. The Tarahumara were kind, but I felt intrusive.

I asked Arturo how we should pay for our visit. He said we could offer a small amount to whomever we photographed or talked to. I suggested that we put our funds together and let the Tarahumara allocate. Arturo picked up a small clay pot and we dropped in pesos.

Before returning to the pickup truck, Arturo led us to a cave, once lived in, higher up on the hill. It provided the barest of shelter, but here in the desert, it seemed a mansion.

Arturo drove along the river then stopped. We followed him down the steep bank to the riverbed, climbing over boulders. We walked

upstream, following the river on smooth river stones. Vertical red cliffs cupped us like two enormous hands. Arturo pointed out an eagle's nest. A young eagle, not mature, but not an eaglet either, circled overhead.

Two boys were fishing in the river with a spool and line, using dough for bait. They had chosen a spot where the river took a twist, where large boulders nearly damned the river and created a pool. We climbed out on a large granite rock. There was a clear pool about fifteen feet below. We could see the fish swimming in a school, but the boys had no luck.

We climbed back up the trail to the road. It was after noon. The sun was overhead. Arturo drove us back to Batopilas. Lunch and cold drinks were in demand. Carmen hardly spoke. She had wilted in the heat. We told Arturo that we would like to go on his mine tour later in the afternoon, but we needed a three-hour rest. He agreed to return to the plaza at 4 o'clock. He said he would show us the finest swimming hole in Batopilas, and we would enter the abandoned San Miguel Mine. He added, "Bring a flashlight."

After a rest, our spirits were refreshed. We clambered back into the truck and drove to the mouth of the mine, a gaping hole, pure rock, large enough for a good-sized truck to enter. Painted on the wall of the mine in red letters was "Do not enter: Dangerous Mine." It was.

Arturo's advice to bring flashlights was the minimum precaution. He knew the mine well. The danger was not from a rock falling. The mine was solid rock, without supports. The danger was that it appeared to be safe. About twenty yards from the mouth of the mine, at a point where one still felt comfortable about entering, and when your eyes were still adjusting to the the darkness, there was a shaft that dropped twenty feet. And, it was nearly as wide as the floor of the cave. We crossed that shaft on a two-foot ledge.

We followed Arturo in single file. He led us past shafts and drifts. One shaft was filled with crystalline water. He told us to be silent then he pitched a stone into the water. Though the stone was falling through the water, we could hear its sound as it tumbled and bounced off the shaft's walls as it fell to the bottom. He then led us to the *veta*, a silver-lead vein. There was silver. It was just a matter of the cost of mining versus the price per ounce.

Arturo told us to be still and turn off our flashlights. It seemed to get colder with the lights out. In the black silence no one stirred. We waited in suspense. Someone in the dark spoke sharply, "Get your hands off!" We burst out laughing, and the flashlights came back on.

Amber felt claustrophobic in spite of the large tunnels. She was happy to leave the mine.

Arturo directed us back down the canyon from the San Miguel Mine. He crossed a bridge, drove the truck off the road and up the

left side of the riverbank. He stopped. Women were washing their laundry. "It's upstream from Batopilas. The water is safe and clean," he said.

We felt like a swim, but caution ruled. Arturo picked up a smooth river stone and skipped it across the river. We all got into this childhood sport. Arturo was champ.

We agreed to meet in the plaza at 7:30 p.m. for dinner. Heidi recommended the Swinging Bridge Restaurant. "They have live music and cold beer," she said.

At dinner I ordered arrachera, a thin-cut Mexican steak. But the cut, influenced by tourists I suspect, was thick. I mentioned to Heidi that I had spent Day of the Dead in San Miguel de Allende.

Heidi asked, "Did you pass a hacienda called La California?"
"I filmed it," I said. "I know Rosalia Peña." Heidi had dated Rosalia's brother Martin.

La California is an architecturally eclectic hacienda, a mini-Hearst Castle, inspired by places that Casimiro Peña, the patriarch of the family, visited while traveling around the world. He named the hacienda for his alma mater, Cal Poly, in San Luis Obispo, California. For the second time, six degrees of separation turned into one.

The conjunto (three-piece band) arrived. An American, Lynn, came to our table and introduced herself. She had a jewelry store in Batopilas, "Open from 4 p.m. to 7 p.m. daily," she said. She told us that the conjunto charged 100 pesos ($9) for three songs.

I called the conjunto over and requested a few songs. They played Norteño style, a polka-beat rhythm. Arturo asked Heidi to dance. Heidi sprang up and I don't recall them sitting down. A young man came over and spoke with Amber. She practiced her Spanish, and he asked her to dance. I enjoyed watching couples dance and listening to the band, then, feeling worn out from sun and activity and knowing that the next morning the bus would leave at 5 a.m. for Junction where I could connect to Guachochi. I waved good night.

Expenses: Hotel Juanita $20, meals $41, tours and tips $20, music $9. Total: $90.

DAY 10
Junction

Bus Journey across Mexico

I woke before the alarm went off. I reached for my glow-in-the-dark-clock and read the time, 4:05. In the coal-black night I got out of bed, felt the wall, found the bathroom and switched on the light.

I left Juanita's at 4:30 a.m., early for the bus. I crossed the plaza and walked to the church. The night was cold and crisp, and faint stars salted the black sky. The deep canyon walls obscured the moon and allowed me to see only a slice of the night sky.

Two shadows approached the church; Carmen and Einar joined me. Arturo, Heidi and Amber showed up a little later. Arturo had risen early and came to say good-bye.

It was a three-hour ride to Junction. Instead of the canyon vista that we saw on the way in, bus headlights now lighted a steep dirt road. We were all quiet. I rocked and swayed with movement of the bus until I slumbered. I woke a little muddled. We were in snow! The road was pure white and framed with pine trees. All the lower branches were covered in white powder. I almost said, "Look at the snow." But I recovered my senses. We were on a white, dusty road. It was pure calcium carbonate, and the dust kicked up by vehicles had powdered the pine branches. It was a beautiful sight until the white road changed to brown.

I got off at Junction and said good-bye to Carmen, Einar, Heidi and Amber. They were returning north to Creel. I was headed south to Guachochi.

There was a roadside home and business at Junction. I had a two-hour wait for the Camion Rojo (Red Bus) to Guachochi. A window to the cafe was open. I called, "Hola"

75

(hello). I heard the shuffing of a chair, and a woman came to the window. I ordered coffee; she invited me into her home. She brought me a cup of hot water, a tablespoon, a jar of Nescafé and a paper napkin.

The room had a cement floor, pink walls, with blue trim. It was a dining room, children's playroom, and storage for oil and transmission fluid. There was a three-week-old newspaper and parking for a child's bike. The walls were decorated with five calendars, each with a different picture and a black velvet painting of three roses and a verse from First Timothy 2:5: *"For there is one God, and one mediator between God and men, the man Christ Jesus."*

Personal treasures, knickknacks, figurines and religious items were

housed in a cupboard. There was a four-foot half-wall that divided the kitchen from this all-purpose room. I could see the glow of the wood-burning, cast-iron kitchen stove. Three children scurried between the kitchen and bedroom, peeking at me as they rushed around. It was a home with joy and love.

I finished my coffee, paid my bill and walked outdoors to wait for the Red Bus.

The Red Bus picked me up at the Junction at 10 a.m. We arrived in Guachochi at 1:30 p.m.

Guachochi was a frontier town, dusty streets, a log cabin restaurant, cowboys and Indians. It reminded me of Gallup, New

Mexico, 1974. There was a western flavor and a Tarahumara presence.

I entered the Tarahumara Artesania (arts and crafts) shop. Cipriano showed me three rooms filled with handcrafts. He said that Guachochi was the center for Tarahumara crafts. He picked up a drum, narrow in width but two feet in diameter, and took it outside. He called to a young Tarahumara man and encouraged him to play the drum. The man smiled, but kept away. Cipriano banged on the

drum. He said he opened the store thirty-four years ago, started with cowboy hats. He had a good location on the center plaza.

I thanked Cipriano and explained that all I could carry was my shoulder bag. I said I had to find a hotel, and he pointed the way to the Melina Hotel.

As I entered the Melina Hotel, a huge wall photograph of a cascading waterfall greeted me. At $30 a night for a very attractive room, it was the best so far. I asked about the photo. "That's

Tónachi," I was told. It was only 40 km (25 miles) from Guachochi, but an hour's drive.

My belief that there is always music, processions, pageantry, fairs and fiestas in Mexico, and that you never need to plan for activities, was confirmed. I arrived on the first day of the fair. Tonight there would be a Norteño band, a dance and the crowning of Miss Guachochi.

It was a modest fair. It seemed like the carnival that came to my hometown in Colorado in the 1950s. I attended the dance and sat as far away from the amplified music as possible. The band played but the room echoed, and music blended into noise. The princesses sat on a dais. The ceremony started late. I was tired so I left without knowing which beauty became queen.

My bus would not leave until 11:30 a.m. the next day. I thought I might be able to sneak in a side trip. I asked a taxi driver what it would cost to make a quick trip to Tónachi. "500 pesos," ($45), he said, for the ride, one way. He didn't seem interested in talking about a round trip with time for photos. Although I felt the price was high, at least I had some idea of the cost.

Expenses: Hotel Melina $30, meals $12, buses $16, entertainment $23. Total: $81.

DAY 11
Tónachi to Parral

Bus Journey across Mexico

I awakened early. The hotel restaurant wasn't open so I ate Marias (vanilla wafer cookies) and drank bottled water for breakfast.

I walked to the taxi stand. It was vacant. It was 7:30 a.m., and since the Tónachi bus operates only three days a week, a taxi was my only choice, or so I thought.

A fellow pulled up in front of the *tortilleria* across from the taxi stand. He was driving a 1984 white Chevy pickup with a black hood, and a green right fender. Steel posts and wooden stakes fenced in the pickup truck bed.

I asked, "Where can I get a taxi?"

"Here's a taxi." He said he hauled pigs, goats, cows and firewood, and he'd take me. His name was Lucas. He was a solid five feet nine inches and was gifted with personality. He could have passed for older brother of the boxer I met ten days ago on the bus to Santa Ana. His salt-and-pepper hair was cut short. He wore cowboy boots, white jeans with a western belt, and a black jacket.

We struck a bargain. I'd pay him the standard $45 taxi fare, and he'd take me to the falls, point out the sites and get me back in three hours.

We talked all the way to Tónachi. We stopped near a Tarahumara lumber mill, in front of a monolith stone where

81

a niche had been carved out for a large statue of the Virgin of Guadalupe. Then we stopped at a second shrine. It was a cave along the riverbank, also with a statue of the Virgin of Guadalupe.

We forded two shallow streams; the tires kicked up a spray of water.

A bridge with massive stone supports was under construction at the first river. I felt like I was back in the woods along the Truckee River near Lake Tahoe. Lucas stopped for me to take pictures of Tónachi, the church and the "laundry." Clothes, all in brilliant colors, were drying over a chain link fence.

We drove past Tónachi, into the river onto a rock pan. Lucas said, "This is the dry season." We walked on the blue-gray rock pan towards the falls. Instead of one giant, wide cascade, as I had seen in the photo, there were three narrow, smaller, falls, like white ribbons tumbling in the sun.

I took a number of photos. I stood where, in the photo in Hotel Melinda, a torrent cascaded. A front view would have taken us on a long route; we did not have time.

Lucas looked for an open store on our way through Tónachi. On the way back, we stopped at the Consupo, the government discount store. It was like an old general store. A counter cut the room off from the merchandise. All the stock was behind the counter stacked on shelves.

Lucas asked for tuna and a man at a counter brought him a can. Lucas had purchased a stack of hot tortillas just before meeting me on the street. Now he finally had something to roll inside his tortilla.

Lucas dropped me off at Hotel Melinda just before 11 a.m. I caught the Transportes Ballezare for Parral. It was a Third Class bus. We stopped frequently. Anyone who waved halted the bus and boarded. The driver, Daniel, left the bus door open for the breeze. He said that Third Class buses are shorter, and this one did seem like a truncated school bus.

I had been on many Mexican buses in the early 1990s, some jammed so tight that holding on was both unnecessary and impossible. But on those trips I never found, or even thought about, body odor. But as we stopped and picked up Tarahumara families, I noticed that soap and cologne would be luxuries for these desert nomads.

The road turned and a rock cliff, like the bow of a ship, divided the highway into two canyons. Daniel slowed and pulled over. Soldiers with dogs ordered us out. They were polite and firm; this was not unusual. Buses, trucks and cars on the highway are frequently checked for drugs, weapons and contraband. Daniel opened the luggage compartment; a soldier prodded the bags. A dog sniffed us then was taken inside the bus and led up and down the aisle. We were waved back on and continued our journey.

I arrived in Parral, checked into Hotel Adriana, 375 pesos ($34). The lobby was marble, and in the entry there was a table with a spray of flowers. I was told it was the best downtown hotel. It was

near the plazas, the cathedral and two museums. But before going out, I got a shoeshine. I purposely wore leather-walking shoes so from time to time I could sit in a plaza, have my shoes shined, talk and ask questions. But I had not seen one shoeshine stand on my entire trip, so I'd accumulated eleven days of dirt and dust.

Expenses: Hotel Adriana $34, meals $13, side trip $45, bus $7, miscellaneous $5. Total: $104.

DAY 12
Parral, Parades and Pancho Villa

Bus Journey across Mexico

There is only one real reason to visit Parral: Pancho Villa. Pancho Villa was ambushed and killed here on July 20, 1923. He is a national hero, the pride of Chihuahua, and he is venerated in Parral. A plaque on the wall at Hotel Tourista commemorates the building as the site of the 1959 celebration that honored Pancho. In the Parral cemetery, his tomb is a monument tended by a distant cousin.

Pancho is both a Saul-Paul and a David-Goliath figure in Mexico. His early life was banditry, but he redeemed himself, joining Francisco Madero in opposing Porfirio Diaz, Mexico's long dominant President. Pancho distinguished himself with military prowess and leadership. He led the Division of the North commonly called "Los Dorados," the Golden Ones. His marching song was La Cucaracha. He held the distinction of having invaded the U.S. with his raid on Columbus, New Mexico, in 1916, the only foreign attack on U. S. soil from the time of the War of 1812 until the terrorist assault on New York City. His small force was chased by General Pershing for over a year but was never caught. Mexicans take pride, not in the raid, but in the U.S.'s inability to capture Pancho. The corrido song La Persecución de Villa (The Pursuit) commemorates the chase.

Parral is a city of clustered hills, with a dozen bridges spanning the serpentine river that snakes through the heart of Parral and made my hotel the center of a labyrinth. Each time I left my hotel I got lost. Once I ended up in a cul-de-sac. When I thought I was taking a walk around a block, I ended up on top of a hill looking over the city.

It surprised me that although Juan Rangel discovered silver here over 350 years ago, the city showed few signs of colonial wealth. There were a few scattered buildings, perhaps 19th century, of notable beauty and architecture, but aside from the church, you would think nothing occurred here before independence from Spain in 1821.

Nuestra Señora de Guadalupe, the brownstone cathedral, had magnificent stained glass windows in vibrant colors. Two major stories were pictured in the glass panels: the story of Christopher Columbus' discovery of the New World and the story of Juan Diego, the Indian who saw the apparition of the Virgin of Guadalupe, the patron saint of Mexico. In Mexico they say, "Even an atheist is a Guadalupano."

The Christopher Columbus stained glass did surprise me because Columbus is generally not praised or considered worthy of honor in Mexico. He is not a national hero. I once taught a U.S. citizenship class, and many students were from Mexico and Latin America, with one from Cuba. When I wrote historic dates on the blackboard, I expected everyone to recognize 1492. But to my surprise, the class drew a blank. October 12th did resonate since Mexico celebrates that date as Día de La Raza, the Day of the New Race, the *mestizo*, the fusion of European and native peoples. A great deal of Mexican history has been editorialized in murals, often portraying the negative aspects of the Spanish conquest. The traveler can see these murals in virtually every town by visiting the Municipal, the City Hall.

I visited the Pedro Alvarado Museum, a mansion built in 1903 as the home of Pedro Alvarado, a wealthy miner, and his family. The mansion's harmony of Classical, Roman, and Byzantine elements has been completely restored and the interior furnished with period pieces. It remained the family home until 2000, when the heirs sold the property to the state. There were amazing photos of the mansion's restoration, showing both the before and after.

Pictures taken in 2000 showed extreme decay and neglect, yet a granddaughter lived there on the lower floor. In places, pigeon excrement built up on the roof two feet thick, and there were photos of men shoveling the guano into bags. The roof leaked and ruined murals on the second floor. I was bewildered that a once-wealthy family, through pure neglect, or lack of funds, had permitted an architectural treasure to suffer years of water damage.

I spent two days in Parral, two days of side-by-side holidays, Día de Los Niños (Day of the Children) and Día del Labor (Mexico's Labor Day). I needed the rest, and this was the perfect spot. I took short walks. There were a number of plazas where I could just sit and watch. I enjoyed the Day of the Children, with its parade of floats. Every conceivable commercial cartoon character waved to the crowds of lining the parade route. The children waved with long, slender balloons that looked like light sabers from Star Wars. Mexicans love the Virgin of Guadalupe and children.

Because it was a holiday, the city came to a commercial halt, but the museums were open. I took a tour of the city in a mini-tourist train. A tractor, fitted to look like a locomotive, pulled tourists in open-air cars around the city center while a guide explained the history and pointed out places of interest.

Pancho was born Doroteo Arango. When he was sixteen, he assaulted the *hacendero*, who may have raped his sister, and fled. For the next twenty years, Doroteo was a bandit and cattle rustler, and he changed his name to Pancho Villa. But when he took up arms for Francisco Madero, the intellectual leader of the 1910 Revolution, Pancho became a hero in the eyes of his people. In the

90

taking of Ciudad Juarez and Zacatecas, Pancho showed that he was a brilliant military leader. Pancho Villa's granddaughter, Rosa Helia Villa Mebius, told me that her grandfather became a symbol of pride as the underdog who baffled General Pershing.

In 1920, Pancho retired. He accepted a hacienda-ranch south of Parral and gold from Mexico's government in payment for his services and promised to stay out of politics. He lived there with multiple wives, children and loyal followers. Pancho became a rancher and a capitalist. He apparently felt secure after three years and, although he traveled with bodyguards, his habits betrayed him, and he was ambushed and killed.

The prize of Parral was the Pancho Villa Museum. It was not large, but was located in the building from where Pancho was ambushed and assassinated in 1923. The museum gave a complete history of Pancho's life and an incredibly detailed list of Pancho's twenty-five wives and twenty-four children. I once met Manuel Arango, a businessman, and asked him if he was related. He said, "I don't know, but Pancho had a very fast horse."

The museums offered a change of pace, and I enjoyed a day of relaxation. I took refreshment at Jesus's stand across from the central plaza. A young Tarahumara girl of thirteen, Juanita, ordered a filled bun. She was a student who wished to become a teacher. I asked if I could take her picture. She said yes. We crossed the street, and I took her photo.

Expenses: Hotel Adriana $34, meals $14, museums and train tour $4. Total: $52.

DAY 13
Anxious to Reach Zacatecas

Bus Journey across Mexico

Before I left Parral, I visited "Panteón de Dolores," the cemetery, and said good-bye to Pancho Villa at his tomb. Pancho rests unquietly, as his remains are incomplete. In 1926, Pancho's grave was desecrated, his body removed and his head severed. His skull was never recovered. It's rumored that Prescott Bush, the patriarch of the Bush family, paid $25,000 for Pancho's head and presented it to Yale's Skull and Bones. When I mentioned this to my friend Santiago, he told me the following story:

A young American, fresh out of law school, came to visit Mexico and was in Parral's plaza when a Mexican with a bag called him with a hiss and motioned for him to step over to a quiet and secluded spot. "Gringo," he said, "would you like to buy Pancho Villa's head?" Cautiously, the Mexican opened the bag and showed the gringo the skull. The young attorney bought the skull, considered it a prize, took it home and placed it on bookshelf in his office and for many years showed it to friends and clients.

Thirty years later, the now older man, wishing to retrace an adventure of his youth, returned to Mexico and Parral. As he visited the plaza a man hissed, "Gringo," called him over to a quiet, secluded spot and showed him a bag. "Would you like to buy Pancho Villa's head?" He carefully opened the bag and showed the gringo a small skull.

The gringo, agitated and somewhat miffed, said, "I own Pancho Villa's head. I bought it right here thirty years ago. What you're trying to sell is a fake, besides look how small it is."

The Mexican said, "I don't doubt you, but this no fake. It **is** Pancho Villa's head! It's small because it's his skull when he was a child!"

I was refreshed, but anxious to arrive in Zacatecas. I told friends and family that I thought I'd cover the Tijuana-Zacatecas route in ten days. Here I was on day thirteen and still hadn't reached Zacatecas.

At Hotel Adriana I asked the desk clerk to check the bus schedules for me. It was eight hours on my AAA map, but that's driving a

95

car. I was hoping to make it in nine hours by bus.

I was surprised by an inconvenient schedule. The direct Parral-Zacatecas bus left daily at 2 p.m. I would have a long morning before I left and then a late arrival. Parral-Durango-Zacatecas, my original route, gave me a choice of 5, 6, or 7 a.m. departures. It was a five-hour trip to Durango, and then I'd have to make a connection for Zacatecas.

I let the sun wake me up and arrived at the bus terminal at 6:30 a.m. I was the first to buy a ticket and requested the front passenger window seat. I took the Transportes Chihuahuense, First Class, but with six short stops and a couple of roadside flag downs.

We headed south and passed the turnoff to Pancho Villa's hacienda at Canutillo, now a national museum. The strangest ruin in Canutillo is a tall, smooth granite wall now used as part of a corral. It's said that the corral was once a jai ali court where Pancho smacked balls against the granite wall.

My seatmate was Sister Lourdes, who was dressed in her white and brown habit. She said she was a cloistered nun, dedicated to a

contemplative life at Nuestra Señora de la Soledad Convent in Sombrerete. I asked how many nuns were in the convent and how they supported themselves. She said, "We are fifteen. We have a schedule, morning mass, two hours of prayer, and we make *rompote* (alcoholic eggnog) and *membrilla de miel* (quince jelly) for sale."

We pulled into Sombrerete. Sister Lourdes said there would be a celebration tonight in honor of the Santa Cruz (Holy Cross) and a three-day festival. We said good-bye, and I had two seats to myself.

The scenery was ranch country, cowboys on horses and herds of cattle. Slowly the ranches gave way to more cacti. I dozed. When I awoke the bus was on a straightaway. Like many Mexican highways, the roadbed was elevated and the road's shoulder steep. A blowout could be fatal. The bus whizzed by three crosses that marked a tragedy. I once wondered why crosses marked traffic deaths. "Why not crosses in homes or bedrooms?" I asked a friend.

"It's not the place, it's the circumstance," I was told. "The unexpected death means a death without a final confession and forgiveness of sins. When you pass a cross, say a prayer for the soul in purgatory."

We pulled into Durango at 2 p.m. Durango is a large city, and I've read that it has an attractive colonial center. But I was eager to reach Zacatecas. I had one hour to catch the bus, just enough time to walk to McDonald's, get a little breather and then back on the bus. In my mind, it was perfect timing.

The sun dipped below the horizon, and gold morphed into black as the Durango bus pulled into the Zacatecas terminal.

I caught a taxi. The driver suggested Hotel Condesa. It was a perfect location, with an even better price, $35 a night. Some of the old hotels, in this case 130 years old, are remodeled and modern, are in great locations and are economical but without parking, which is why the price is thrifty.

97

I checked in, washed up, and by 9 p.m. I was ready for a walk to shake the feeling of the bus seat's indentation off my backside. I stepped outside into a nighttime photographer's paradise.

A rainbow of multicolored dancing waters illuminated a plaza fountain. Cars passed under a floodlit ancient aqueduct. Light

accented an 18th century bullring that had been converted by an architectural masterstroke into a dream hotel. Arched portals were lit from below, church facades highlighted and the cathedral, carved in pink-rose cantera stone was splashed in light.

When I visited in 1992, Zacatecas was a gem, now it was polished to a brilliant multifaceted cut diamond. "Mexico begins in Zacatecas," I've told my friends. On the map, it's close to the geographical center, and that's where it should be; it is the heart of Mexico.

Somewhere after I left Durango, I crossed an imaginary line, like Dorothy opening the door after the tornado dropped her house in Oz. She saw the world turn from black and white to Technicolor. That's how I felt. I left behind inelegant, dusty, dingy, worn towns and battered pickup trucks and was magically set down in a vortex of energy, quality, luxury, and colonial 18th and 19th century architectural beauties carved in rose-pink cantera stone.

In Zacatecas, a UNESCO World Heritage site, there was an unsurpassed Baroque *churrigueresco* detailed cathedral and world-class museums, with Picassos, Goyas, Dalís and Monets. The entire city was a cultural collection and a walker's town, with art galleries, museums, libraries and bookstores, coffee shops and luxury goods. Crafts and souvenirs were art treasures.

Tourists drive into Mexico, see a border town, buy a trinket and return home repelled by the wrong end of the magnet. If only they would take the toll road south to Zacatecas. To me it was like leaving Laramie, Wyoming, in 1950 for California. You just had to drive across a thousand miles of desert and dust to reach paradise.

Here the streets were not paved in California gold, but in smooth, square cantera stones. Unlike cobblestones that shake your kidneys or economy asphalt, the flat, cantera stones provided a smooth ride and added charm, class and a sense of timeworn history. In the morning rush, police directed traffic. Cars moved among the narrow streets instead of trucks loaded with workers, which I had become accustomed to seeing in Chihuahua.

There was only one reason to visit Parral, Durango: Pancho Villa. There is no reason to leave Zacatecas.

My room at Hotel Condesa overlooked the Teatro, the Cathedral and the Bufa. As I opened my eyes and stirred at 7 a.m., I heard the roar of a cannonade salute. Soaring rockets opened this day of celebration in honor of Día de la Santa Cruz (Day of Holy Cross). It was *festival*.

When I first visited Zacatecas twenty years ago, I came for the annual festival celebrating the "Battle between the Moors and the Christians." It's a 400-year-old tradition that lasts for a week, and thousands participate. It's pure medieval pageantry: King Charlemagne and Turks, ladies-in-waiting, clashing armies, drums and cannon fire, marches and faux battles. Michelin likely would

100

give it "Worth the Journey" rating. In 1992 speaking Spanish was, if not a must, very helpful. Today, the hotel bellboy is likely to speak better English than the hotel owner. In remote villages, someone is likely to have worked in El Norte and now speaks English.

I took morning photos while the traffic was light and quickly discovered that my second memory card was full. My gut wrenched when the best photo shop in town couldn't transfer the contents of my billion-mega-byte-Fuji card to a CD. No studio in Zacatecas could, but Sanborn's sold me a 256-mega-byte card for $85. I paid $70 for the billion-mega-byte model.

The Toma de Zacatecas (Taking of Zacatecas) refers to the battlefield success of the Division del Norte led by Pancho Villa, but today I felt taken ... taken by the beauty of the city. Pancho's statute was atop La Bufa, the backdrop of Zacatecas, a colorado-red monolith rising above the city, looking like the petrified humpback of some gigantic Jurassic stegosaurus that had yet to be excavated. From La Bufa there was a *teleferico* (overhead cable car) that rode above the city for an eagle's view and took you to La Mina Eden, the source of mining millions and the best mining tour I've ever taken.

The Teatro was a 19th-century opera house with tiered galleries and stained glass windows. Every Thursday the Municipal Band played on the steps in front of the Teatro. The program ended with "La Marcha de Zacatecas." The orchestra and the public stood. Children, the youngest members of the band, were invited one-by-one to take the conductor's baton and lead the band in playing their city's patriotic song.

I sat with the crowd on the Teatro steps, my knees hunched up. A discarded candy wrapper floated past, landed in front of the band and danced, moved by invisible currents of wind while I listened to the variety program. The orchestra played a Spanish Paso Doble, La Bamba, Tequila, Solamente Una Vez and of course, La Marcha de Zacatecas. I had arrived.

Expenses: Hotel Condesa $34, meals $10, buses $41, taxi $3. Total: $88.

Visit to El Museo Zacatecano (Zacatecan Huichol Museum)

The Huichol Art and Textile Collection in Zacatecas is home to 166 wall hangings, which appear simple but they incorporate a plethora of symbols, both in design and color. The wall hangings are about twenty inches square and are displayed under glass. I photographed them with a hand-held camera without a flash. I tried to avoid glare but in some cases it was impossible.

In the downstairs lobby there was a display of beaded items for sale. A Huichol man and his son were patiently working on their art. Blazing in color from the stairwell leading to the museum, there is an eighty-panel beaded mosaic, which is called the Huichol Bible, or Mystic World View. It is the glory of the museum.

Huichols are known for brilliantly colored bead and yarn  "paintings." These paintings are often psychedelic visions influenced by peyote and interpreted by shamans. They contain pre-Hispanic religious elements, and in a religious context they are considered transcendental, interior visions.

José Acevedo Alvarez, a quiet man, was sitting on a wicker chair when I entered the Huichol textile museum room. I assumed he was security, a job requiring patience for a long day of little activity. But he surprised me with his personal background and a depth of knowledge that would require a book to record.

He introduced himself. "My father was Spanish and fifteen and my Huichol mother was twelve when they married. Father was a miner, and the Huichols banished my mother. My parents saved and bought goats and cattle. But we children never went to school." José said that he had married and raised nine children. Although he had no schooling, all of his children were educated and two went to college. He said, "I came to Zacatecas and I learned. I learned how to dress and how to speak with people." In every sense he displayed courtesy and a keen intelligence.

José became my guide to the textile collection. He called the Huichol textiles on display *mantas*, blankets in my vocabulary, but better translated as tapestries. José pointed out the textiles. "Three colors are dominant: green (nature) red (energy, life force) and black (death)." He mentioned the beaded mosaic in the stairwell, "That's the Huichol Bible," he said. "Our history and beliefs are recorded there."

I was curious about the beads, which are called *chiquira*. "When did the beaded art begin?"

"In 1935," he said, "Enrique Mertens, a Belgian physician, brought beads to the Huichols as a substitute for yarn in their 'paintings.'" He took me to a case. "This is our oldest example." It was a bowl and beads were strung on a string and glued to it. "Artisans found the beaded strings difficult to work with. Curves posed a particular problem; spaces were not filled in as with yarn. The design and color had to be thought out before threading the string. The solution was to place beads individually, then to set them in *campeche* glue mixed with beeswax."

I turned my attention back to the textiles, "Are they sewed together," I asked, "like a quilt?"

"No, they are hung on the wall. They adorn a sacred place."

"Cloth *retablos*," I thought.

"Every cloth includes a design flaw," José said and pointed out a mistake. Like a Middle Eastern carpet, they incorporated imperfection. "The artisan's signature is a coded message known only to the artisan and the shaman," José explained.

He told me that Huichols associate the scorpion with a parched spring, bad harvest and an increase of these venomous insects. But a wet spring brings snakes and an abundant harvest; hence, Huichols revere snakes and scorn scorpions.

He explained symbols in the designs. José said that Tata, the sun, was the supreme source of energy, everlasting, in the past, the present and the future. Deer were messengers to the gods. Christians would call them angels. Lizards were vigilant (watchers) for the sacred spirits.

The Three Sacred Spirits

1. Man, Tatuche, is often seen with a deer's tail.

2. Light-Shadow, Tatehuari, is the interplay of light and shadow. (Black is used in textile design to create the effect of an optical inversion like the negative of a photograph.)

3. Woman, Tacuche, is often portrayed as transformed into an animal form.

If a Huichol encounters a stranger, he will address him as "Tata." It's a sign of respect as if to say "you are greater than I am." A Huichol, if addressed diminutively, "Huicholito," will feel insulted.

I looked at the designs. Each one teased my sight with a notion of symmetry that did not exist.

I was astonished to learn that Huichol beadwork, based on textile designs, was a major art form and had been inspired by a European. The museum room was dedicated to Enrique Mertens.

I asked José about the huge mural over the staircase. It could have been the Mad Hatter's checkerboard. It covered the wall and was made up of eighty individual panels, ten panels across and eight high, each about a foot square. A sign said that the artists used over two million beads in the mural. It was titled: "Visión de un Mundo Místico (Mystic World View).

From a distance, the mural looked like a tapestry exploding in color, as if the artist was inspired by a picture of a supernova or wished to create a symbolic view of the Big Bang. It appeared to be a random mosaic of millions of scrambled, scattered beads acting as the background for childlike stick-figure drawings of animals, plants, flowers and snakes. But a closer view brought the chaos into a new focus. Like peering into a microscope and adjusting the lens, it became clear that the art was intentional and organized. José said, "It's the Huichol Bible."

"The mural was both a religious and cultural record, like Genesis and the Book of Chronicles," I thought.

José pointed out the Supreme Vital Force, the Creation, the Flood and the Mystery of Three Sacred Spirits coming from one Supreme Force. A line of deer, the equator of the mural divided the composition, horizontally. "Deer are messengers," José said. "Christians would call them angels." My eyes followed the two serpents, which looked like trails passing through different mosaic squares. "That's the story of the Flood, a new beginning (re-creation)." Huichols believed that after the Flood, Huichols and sustenance (beans, corn and squash) were created.

The center, which at first looked like one mosaic, was made of four squares, balanced light and dark. José said, "The Bible is divided into two parts, left and right, good and evil, drought and abundance, birth and death. Each side has forty panels." One needed to focus and concentrate, to come close and then back off, to see squares within squares like chapters and paragraphs, patterns within patterns. The mosaic was visually like Russian nesting dolls.

The imagery and artistry were complex, with each drawing being iconic. "Within the good there is evil," José said and commented on the black figure of death within the good half of the mural. Likewise, the wicked side had a subtext of benevolence as if to warn the good of the potential for evil and to instill hope among the wicked for benevolence.

José continued. "The left side represents the male, whose symbol is the scorpion. It represents scarcity, darkness and evil. The right side, the female side, is represented by the firefly (glow worm). It brings abundance, light and good. The mural recorded pre-Hispanic beliefs in contemporary art. It mirrored the Huichol community's heart and soul. José explained and pointed. The sacred disk at the center of the mural represented Tepari, Vital Energy. There were symbols for the four elements: air, water, fire and earth. The mural also contrasted two epochs, drought and rain. As I examined the complex art, it became clearer.

I recalled the childhood nursery rhyme: "There Was a Man," which encouraged a second look when something was difficult to understand.

There was a man in our town,
And he was wondrous wise,
He jumped into a bramble bush,
And scratched out both his eyes;
But when he saw his eyes were out,
With all his might and man,
He jumped into another bush,
And scratched 'em in again.

DAY 14
San Luis Potosí : Arrival

Bus Journey across Mexico

I boarded an Ominbus, which took me directly from Zacatecas to San Luis Potosí in cool, swift comfort. For 114 pesos ($11), Omnibus covered the 191 km (115 miles) in just over two hours.

I've told family and friends, "If I had to choose, right now, where to live in Mexico, I'd make it San Luis Potosí." It's Mexico's geographical heart. It's an historic, colonial, cultural and university center. It's a large city with the feel and ambiance of a cultured small town. But what I like most is how close San Luis Potosí is to side trips, places of cultural, historic and ecological interest.

Real de Catorce, the desert ghost-mining town is three hours north. Xilitla, Edward James's surrealist garden, is east over the mountains in the Huasteca, where you'll find a paradise of waterfalls, rivers, scuba diving in mineral springs and lush vegetation. You can make a day trip to Queretaro, or Zacatecas, or San Miguel de Allende, or Guanajuato or Dolores Hidalgo.

If you feel you must find a beach, try the hot springs resort at Gogorrón. There is no beach; there is no sand, but you'll have large pools, thermal baths, green grass and shade trees.

The locals say, "It's the five-hour city," meaning it's a five-hour drive from San Luis Potosí to the major commercial and industrial markets: Mexico City, Guadalajara, and Monterrey.

But for me San Luis Potosí is the city of three-hour side trips, where one can enjoy a day trip and experience a sense of awe, marveling at the extraordinary variety and diversity of enjoyable places to visit and people to meet.

111

1. Local Excursions: A twenty-mile drive south of San Luis Potosí will take you back a century, to haciendas, a rural life, with donkey-drawn alfalfa carts and horse-drawn vendors of fresh water in barrels, cows and chickens running in the streets and pigs rooting in shallow streams.

You can soak and delight in the healing waters of the nearby hot springs at Gogorrón.

Haciendas, (Jarral de Berrios, Bledos, Carranco, La Ventilla, Gogorrón) are clustered for an easy visit and spectacular photography. Some haciendas are neglected and appear abandoned. Jarral de Berrios is a fairy tale scene with conical stone structures, columns and towers. Others are maintained as vacation homes and used as movie sets. All add to a sense of history and the significance of a once imperial aristocracy.

2. North: Real de Catorce is the well-preserved mining town, which you enter through a one-way mile-long tunnel at the 9000-foot level in the Sierra Madre Mountains.

Here you can join a group on horseback that will bring you to even more remote ghost towns and views of the Sierras. Or you can walk the cobblestone streets, sit in the plaza, observe the old stone buildings, hike the winding, terraced streets and gaze at the valleys beyond.

You can visit an ancient cockfight ring built like a small Roman coliseum, find calming serenity in the church of San Francisco, see folk art milagros (miracles), testaments to answered prayers, visit the local museum where silver coins were once minted, wander through an ancient cemetery adorned with bright plastic flowers and dine at La Abundancia, a converted mansion.

3. East: Cresting the Sierra Madre Mountains you'll notice that the brown desert high plateau switches to a lush green profusion, enhanced by rivers and waterfalls.

You've entered La Huasteca, a paradise for picnickers, swimmers and hikers. And if you're willing to make a circle trip and spend a night, you can follow the Corridor of Missions, five elaborate folk-churrigueresque, polychrome, churches built by Father Junípero Serra before he was called to found the missions in California.

You may reserve a night at Hotel El Castillo in Xilitla and visit the magical, surrealistic gardens built by Edward James, which are worth a special journey.

4. South: Dolores Hidalgo is Mexico's Cradle of Independence. It is also the revered site of the spectacular tomb that honors Mexico's foremost Ranchero singer, Jose Alfredo Jimenez. It is also the home to multicolored pottery.

If you don't spend all your time shopping in Dolores Hidalgo, you can visit Mexico's unique tunneled city, Guanajuato.

Here the first battle of the War of Independence was fought in 1810. Today, Guanajuato is famed for the annual cultural event, The Cervantino. Each October, Guanajuato hosts this International Music Festival that attracts musicians, dancers and theater performers from all over the world.

5. Further South, San Miguel de Allende. Less than three hours from San Luis Potosí, you'll discover the artistic, bohemian-inspired, home to over 10,000 expatriates (expats), Americans and Canadians, who have developed an exceptional community of arts, theater, culture and splendid homes that are often opened to the public for tours or charitable fundraisers.

San Miguel de Allende shops carry the best handcrafts of Mexico. Only the size of your suitcase will limit your shopping.

6. Also South: Queretaro boasts plazas, fine restaurants, a Sunday dance in the center plaza, beautiful colonial mansions and churches, a spectacular aqueduct, history around every corner, fine museums, theater and an opera house.

If you stay in Queretaro, consider Hotel Mansion La Marquesa. Then take side trips to Bernal, which is so colorful that you will think of a Hollywood musical set and to Tesquisquiapan with its enormous plaza and curative hot springs.

7. Northwest: Zacatecas. Here is where Mexico begins. If you can only visit one city, make it Zacatecas.

From the El Paso border to Zacatecas, you cross 800 miles of desert, but when you arrive in Zacatecas, it's like Dorothy landing in Oz after a tornado and opening the door of her twisted house, and watching black and white change to color. Zacatecas is Technicolor, a city of colonial beauty, historical importance, medieval pageantry, and it's easy to visit, with world-class museums.

Take a taxi to La Bufa. This is where one should start. See the city from the La Bufa, the rose-colored outcropping shaped like the humped back of a prehistoric stegosaurus, ride the aerial tram that glides over Zacatecas and arrives near the entrance to El Eden, the mine that gushed silver.

Spend a day visiting marvelous museums. There are almost a dozen, from abstract art to popular arts, a mask museum, Huichol religious fabric art, international collections brought to Zacatecas by the Coronel brothers and contemporary art housed in the former Governor's Mansion. Rest and recharge at Café Acropolis, which is an art gallery and museum that occupies a corner of the old classic market in the city's center.

Rose and green cantera stone enhances the beauty of Zacatecas' buildings. Boutiques and restaurants occupy the old central market, which was built of iron girders and columns that reminds one of the Eiffel Tower. The cathedral is a Baroque masterpiece.

A night walk is a must. Zacatecas is a city caressed, adorned and highlighted in a spectacle of light that accents the carved beauty of its buildings, and it glows with multicolored fountains.

Arriving in San Luis Potosí, I purchased a taxi voucher in the bus terminal at a fixed rate of 31 pesos and told the driver, "Hotel Real Plaza." I've been a regular at the Real Plaza for years, since I first taught finance and English at the Mexican Cross Cultural Institute in the mid 1990s. I was immersed in the culture and community, became acquainted with artists, politicians and of course managers and executives, my students. The school closed in 2000 when the owner fell in love and moved to Spain. It's the only time I've ever regretted someone falling in love.

The cab driver was a young man who had worked in Napa Valley, California for three years. "Were you able to save up and bring home some money?" I asked.

He tapped the steering wheel with his hand. "I bought this taxi," he said.

Hotel Real Plaza's posted rate was 640 pesos, but I asked for the "promotional rate" and the price was reduced to 512 ($48) a night. I checked in and went to the tenth floor.

I looked out the window and to my surprise there was a new gated residential development two blocks north. I had to take a closer look. I walked down the ten flights of stairs just for the exercise, walked three blocks north and found the subdivision. There were 103 townhouses; two were for rent. I spoke with a woman who was washing her car in front of her three-bedroom, two-bath townhouse. "Could you give me an idea of the range of prices?"

She said, "Last year I paid 800,000 pesos ($75,000)."

"Location, location, location," is the real estate agent's mantra, and it surely is true about the townhouses at Villa Vallarta. Across from the entrance is La Bodega, a major supermarket. In five minutes, a resident could walk to Parque Tequis and sit in the sun, or read a newspaper in the shade, enjoy the fountains, or meet a friend for coffee at Italian Coffee. It's located on Avenida Carranza, the main thoroughfare where buses arrive frequently.

On a hot day Parque Tequis offers shade, and you can try any of forty-two ice cream or sherbet flavors at Tequisnieves (Tequis

 Snow). It's a couple of doors down from Italian Coffee. Tequisnieves offers many flavors, such as *Springtime, Cinderella's Kiss, Angel's Kiss, Serenade of Love, Moonscape, Wind's Prayer, Song of the Mermaids and 1,000 Flowers.*

Founders Square is a twenty-minute stroll and the center plaza about thirty minutes. You'll find superior restaurants everywhere. For me, it's not the food; the ambiance and music bring me back. Mariachis play at Mi Cocula, and pianists add a soft romantic flavor to Gran Via, Las Flores and La Virreyna restaurants. At El Posole, it's the diners' chatter that is the music. And you'll learn Spanish; there is no noticeable expat community in San Luis

Potosí. You can't even buy the English language Mexican edition of the Herald newspaper in San Luis Potosi.

I looked forward to continuing Bus Journey Across Mexico, Stage Two, San Luis Potosí to Puebla. Puebla was south, but I wanted to see the Huesteca, missions and mines. I would take the bus east to Rio Verde. But I got sidetracked. I headed to San Miguel for the summer to attend Spanish language school.

Expenses: Hotel Real Plaza $48, bus $11, taxi $3, meals $16. Total $78.

Summer School in San Miguel de Allende

Travel is for fun, surprises, education and adventure. Sometimes the best experience comes with a change in plans.

San Miguel de Allende is south of San Luis Potosí. It has a large expat community and is known for art, culture and Spanish language schools. I thought I'd try school for a month and check out the cultural programs.

I signed up for an intensive Spanish course that included room and board with a Mexican family. It was cheaper to pay tuition and stay with a family than to stay in a hotel without going to school. Tuition, room and board: $49 per day.

I arrived on a Friday, just in time for the annual charity Dine-Around where cocktails, dinner and dessert gave the guests an inside view of fabulous homes in San Miguel de Allende. I also arrived in time for the Cinema Shorts and Documentaries that were being shown in a variety of locations in town. Then there was the bullfight with *novilleros* (professionals in training) on Sunday, with all the pomp, ceremony and music, but it's not a spectacle for everyone.

There was a Familiarization Trip for Writers. I was invited to cocktails and dinner held in the Biblioteca (San Miguel's library), which is a cultural center for films, music and painting. The second week the calendar changed from Cinema to Chamber Music. Bellas Artes, in the Miguel Mala Auditorium offered an evening of arias with Fernando Nunez, pianist, and Gabriela Perales, soprano.

But my major joy was the Jardín, San Miguel's plaza where *mariachis* play nightly and the *Tuna* plays on weekends, confirming that Mexico is music.

San Miguel de Allende is an old city. They celebrate Day of the Dead, but there should be a new festival ... the Day of the Almost Dead. Oldsters are everywhere and retirees are moving in. From the balcony of the Teatro Angela Peralta, looking down on the orchestra section, the $40 seats, there is a sea of white heads.

Guanajuato is known for its macabre display of mummies. These are cadavers, whose family or friends failed to pay for a lifetime tomb (strange choice of words, should be an eternal tomb). On being disinterred from their "last resting place" they were found to have been naturally mummified by mineral water seeping into their crypt and are now on view.

San Miguel de Allende's "mummies" visit the Jardín, the central plaza, which is sometimes referred to as Jurassic Park. They are the living almost dead. Mariachis gather and play in the Jardin. But it should be Glen Campbell belting out "Almost Heaven," or a church choir singing "Nearer My God to Thee."

San Miguel's elderly populate art galleries, shops and boutiques. And I was told that, "They are adding to the foreign section at the cemetery." Mexico laughs at itself, "So far from God, so close to the United States." In San Miguel that quip is reversed, "So far from Texas, so near to God."

Million-dollar homes and affordable cooks, maids and gardeners, this is expat Mexico, Gringolandia. People speak of healing and art, "life paths" and a slower pace. There are artists and dilettantes, the real and the pretentious. Mexicans are the hosts; Americans and Canadians are the guests. It's a mix of life and culture. In my mind, it's sculptured in bas-relief.

I sat under the Allende arches at the restaurant at the corner of the Jardín and ordered breakfast, *huevos Mexicanos* (scrambled eggs with diced tomato, pepper and onion). It was just after 7 a.m., and I was their first customer. Pedro, my waiter, brought me a cup of coffee and said, "The cook hasn't arrived."

"That's OK," I said, "her huevos Mexicanos are worth the wait."

Pedro and I chatted. His English was better than my Spanish. He said, "I worked in the U.S. for nine years. There are more Americans in San Miguel de Allende than in Arizona."

Academia Hispano Americano: An Adventure in Education

This Old Gringo thought he should add to his Spanish vocabulary and practice conversation. He's been getting by in Spanish for over forty years but thought it was time to go back to school and get the student experience.

He heard favorable comments about Academia Hispano Americano (AHA), and they had the best brochure and the most professional course outline. He was sold on "Vamos a hablar español (Let's Speak Spanish)." He even liked the name, Aha! It seemed to add a pinch of chile to the program. The schedule was intensive:

Monday through Friday

Mornings:
8:30-9:20 a.m. Grammatical Problems
9:30-11:20 a.m. Intensive Spanish
11:30-12:20 p.m. Conversation

Afternoons:
12:30-1:45 p.m. Novo Hispanic Literature
Lunch break:

3:35-5:00 p.m. Mexican Themes (Civics and Sociology)
5:05-6:20 p.m. History of Mexico

The three afternoon courses were lectures. An hour of grammar didn't seem too bad and the Intensive Spanish referred to as "Vamos a hablar español" offered conversation. The Old Gringo took the placement test. There were five levels, and he was assigned to Level Three.

The teachers were professional, animated, prepared, spoke clearly and took an interest in the students. But for the Old Gringo, there was a surprise. Intensive Spanish meant two more hours a day of grammar: Ser and Estar, Por and Para, Preterit and Co-preterit, that the Old Gringo thought he had learned years ago as the Imperfect Tense.

Where was the hablar? And since he tested at Level Three, the conversation was not a challenge. The literature class nudged his vocabulary forward, and the afternoon lectures added to his knowledge and understanding.

The high school and college students were being well grounded in grammar for a return to classes in the fall. Their writing, already solid, would be superior, but the Old Gringo had expected more spontaneous conversation. And in San Miguel de Allende you had to fight to speak Spanish on the street. Clerks, waiters, shopkeepers often practice their English as foreign students try out Spanish. Even cultural events are largely conducted in English. The Festival Camara de Music (Chamber Music) began with all introductions in English, and when a piano key broke and the program was delayed, the Mexican audience in the upper balcony had to hiss and demand an explanation, chanting, "Español, español, español."

Academia Hispano Americano is academic and professional, but for this student it was not a center for expanding conversational skill. Conversation for most students was with their host families.

The Old Gringo Rearranges His Class Schedule

I don't like grammar. I never liked grammar. I will never like grammar! Spontaneously, eché la pinta (I cut class).

What a great day! I escaped from Academia Hispano Americano, and immediately jumped from the frying pan into the proverbial fire. I tested the truth of that folk wisdom. I jumped into the Warren Hardy School, one I had heard about by word-of-mouth.

Two graduates of the Warren Hardy School, and general remarks from residents of San Miguel de Allende, praised Warren Hardy's school and his method. "It's a brilliant method," I was told, "it's solid, practical and conversational."

My curiosity was whetted, I dropped by the Tourist Office, asked directions to the Warren Hardy School, looked it up on my map, walked a few blocks. I gave the door a solid crack, as instructed by a notice tacked on the door, "Knock loudly."

Mrs. Hardy came to the door. I explained that I had heard of Warren Hardy, the school and the method. I said, "I'd like to know more."
Mrs. Hardy said, "There's a class in session. Let me seat you. Warren is teaching."

So in the few seconds from knocking on the door, feeling the freedom of escape from one class, there I was seated in a Level Two grammar class. What a difference in method.

At the break, Warren sat with me. He's a man of instant rapport and exudes concern for the student. He explained his methods and told me a short history of his teaching background.

One of his first Spanish classes was a group of middle-aged MDs. The immersion method of 100 percent Spanish did not work for them. He noted that the physicians quickly started to compile 3x5 flash cards, Spanish on one side, English on the other.

Warren explained, "The young brain up to about age fourteen is intuitive. But as we mature each side of the brain, right and left, becomes more specific. The adult brain of mature students learns quicker and better by starting with a clear explanation in his own language and then by repetition."

Students work in pairs. The method emphasizes speaking and repetition. Warren is alert to personality and makes sure students are compatible. Teachers are available to fill in if the class is an odd number of students.

Unlike the AHA school, the average age in the class tended to be mature rather than college-aged. In a class of twenty, I noted only three students I thought were under forty.

Warren assigned a teacher as my partner to work on the preterit tense. First Warren lectured at the white board. He described the lesson, and gave examples in English. No one was lost. Then as a group we pronounced the words, the conjugations, and a few sentences. Next we followed step-by-step instructions; some sentences were in English to translate. Later, questions were in Spanish to be answered in Spanish.

The students were remarkably alert, active and communicative. When there were questions, they were asked in English and clarified. At the break several students told me how they had tried a number of times to learn Spanish with little success, but here they felt confident and were progressing.

Warren has a system. The beginner class lasts two and one-half weeks, and he promises that the student will learn a basic vocabulary of 500 practical words and a power vocabulary. He emphasizes learning proper courtesy when speaking and interacting in Mexico. Yet, classes are only nine hours a week. He assigns homework from the workbook. And the workbook explains all exercises in English. No one gets lost. Classes are on alternate days. The student has time to memorize the vocabulary, practice, write the assignments, and see San Miguel de Allende, something grossly lacking in my current (well, former) schedule.

And what's my reward for being a runaway? As always, good luck.

I was hustling back to AHA and the Novo-Hispanic Literature Class, walking fast up Canal Street when I heard my name called out. Camie Sands, who I had met a year before, was racing after me. When she stopped and caught her breath, she invited me to "cocktails and dinner tonight at the Bibliotheca, a Familiarization Tour for Writers to promote San Miguel de Allende."

I accepted her invitation.

Juan Manuel, director of the library, a cultural center of San Miguel de Allende, gave us a tour. The library has over 50,000 books, a patio cafe, an art room for children, and a movie theater. There is a music room dedicated to Quetzalcoatl, with murals painted on all four walls. The children's choir practices there on Saturday mornings, and an adult choir sings on Thursday evenings.

I sat with Juan Manuel, Joyce Wyels, who writes for the *Smithsonian Magazine*, and Mrs. Able, whose Moroccan husband welcomed our group. With such luck, why go to morning grammar classes?

Next morning, I was up at 6:30 a.m. and at Restaurant Jardín for breakfast. At the next table a gentleman with grey hair pulled back and tied in a ponytail sat down, and we began to talk. His name was Artemio Sepulveda. He said he was an artist, and he had just delivered four paintings to Galleria Diana.

He said he grew up in a poor family. They lived in a mining town in northern Mexico, but he had a chance to study in Mexico City at the Bellas Artes in the 1940s. That was the time of the great Mexican muralists, so I asked about Rivera, O'Gorman, Orozco and Siquieros. He knew Rivera and studied with Orozco. To support himself, he modeled for art classes. An agent visited the art school and invited Artemio to model for Siquieros, who had won a contract to paint the mural in Mexico's Central Hospital. "So next time you're in Mexico City," he said, "look for Artemio, the young miner in the mural."

Good luck didn't stop. In the afternoon, tired, thirsty and in need of a beer, I looked for a seat under the arches in the plaza. All the tables were taken, but a single lady occupied one. I asked if she was alone. "Si," she said.

"Could I share a table with you?" I asked. She agreed, and I ordered a beer. I asked her about San Miguel, if she was a resident or a tourist.

She introduced herself, Gabriela Zepeda Garcia Morena, "I'm an archeologist, the director of the dig at La Canada de la Virgin." La Canada is the major archeological site about twenty miles from San Miguel de Allende.

She told me that it would not be opened to the public for another two years. She believed that the site was ceremonial and a center for astronomers and mathematicians because the orientation of the temples and features were aligned with sun and moon cycles.

It was time to go. I called for the bill, thanked Gabriela for allowing me to be her table guest and headed back to AHA for the afternoon lectures on Mexican government and history. I might not like grammar, but AHA lectures were entertaining and informative.

From Gringolandia to Primolandia

Mary Carmen Olvera Trejo, Zacatlan's tourist director, sent me an invitation to the Apple Harvest Festival. I hedged. I was studying Spanish in San Miguel de Allende, known as Gringolandia for its large expat community, and I thought it would be a strain to rush to Zacatlan for a weekend visit. Besides, I was reluctant to return to Zacatlan. Sometimes a second trip spoils the memory of the first.

I had a week to go, and was enjoying the afternoon lectures. Mary Carmen sent a second invitation, "Bernardo Mendez, Consul for Business and Commerce, will be here for the opening." Bernardo was my friend, so I left the school, said good-bye to my host family and headed south to Zacatlan de las Manzanas.

When I arrived at the tourist office Friday evening, Mary Carmen was typing on the computer keyboard and speaking on her cell phone. Without hanging up she told me that we would had to hurry to the presentation of WEY (Nahuatl for Big), a new magazine devoted to the arts. I was expected to say a few words.

On the way across the plaza, I was stopped for an introduction. Since my article "Zacatlan, Mexico's Brigadoon" was published in *Arte y Cultura* I had become a minor celebrity. We tried to rush, but were stopped again and again. Each introduction, handshake and hug was followed by, "Es mi primo (my cousin)." I told Mary Carmen, "This is Primolandia."

At the Casa Cultura, originally a 16th-century convent, I ducked my head under stone archways as we worked our way to a room where five young men would present their new magazine.

When I was called upon, I asked, "Who is Elmer?" One of the five raised his hand. "You took the cover picture?" I asked.

He said, "Yes."

"It is beyond photography." I said, "This is art. Congratulations."

The evening was a blur. I was dazed with names. Everyone seemed to have a title and three names, like "Presidente Municipal Raul Hernandez Quintero."

Although this was the Apple Harvest Festival, an eight-day celebration, Zacatlan's twenty-five indigenous communities took an active role in performances, cuisine and handcrafts. Poems were recited in both Nahuatl and Spanish. Kwaxochitl dominated Sunday. From noon to 10:30 p.m. members from nine different indigenous communities performed on stage in the plaza. Dances, bands, recitations, a short enactment of a courting ritual and the presentation of Celsa "Doncella Kwaxochitl" (Celsa is the Queen of Flowers) represented the indigenous community.

125

Looking over the program, I realized this was a more sophisticated and a much larger event and celebration than I had imagined. There was a rodeo and a bullfight, many bands, singing groups, and TV stars who would perform. There were public dances, fireworks, entertainers, two fashion shows, two religious processions in honor of the Virgen de la Asuncion, and more.

Mary Carmen said, "El Camion Verde (the Green Bus) will pick us up at 7:30 a.m." We were going to Puebla with the indigenous dance group from Xonotla, who would perform "Tetlalpalotl, danza de peticion de mano (courtship dance, asking for the girl's hand)." She assured me that we would return in time for the fair's opening. Bernardo was expected at 6 p.m.

Back at the hotel, I wasn't even unpacked, and I set my alarm for 6:30 a.m.

I arrived in front of the Tourist Office at 7:25 a.m. Dancers were waiting. The Green Bus arrived at 7:54. Forty dancers and two guests boarded. Some of the dancers were on Mexican time. There was shuffling on and off the bus. We left at 8:30 a.m.

The driver immediately took the wrong route; we were headed for Mexico City. "Puebla, Puebla, Puebla!" the dancers shouted. The Green Bus took a 360-degree tour of Zacatlan through narrow streets and tight corners, hampered by one-way streets.

During the two-hour drive to Puebla we were followed by a pickup truck, which carried the dancers' props, rustic wood siding for a house and thatching for a roof, two *guacalotes* (turkeys) and a *borrego* (sheep). Apparently, the courtship would involve a trade.

The police stopped the pickup as we entered Puebla. Live animals were not permitted without a license. We were delayed about fifteen minutes while the police and Mary Carmen talked and confirmed with authorities.

We drove to the heart of Puebla and parked between the plaza and the cathedral. The dancers were happy to get out and change into costumes. The men in the pickup truck started building the stage-set house. The turkeys were picked up and caressed. The sheep was coaxed from the pickup to the street.

The costumed dancers attracted a crowd. They performed twice, once in the main plaza, then a block away at the Casa de Cultura. The house, with its thatched roof, was picked up by the male dancers and carried the distance.

Then it was back on the bus and on the road to Zacatlan. I sat on the jump seat next to the driver. I loved the panoramic view, looking out over the highway.

Back in Zacatlan, I freshened up and looked at the program. The inauguration was scheduled for 6 p.m., Fanaticos del Rock (Rock and Roll Fanatics) at 7 p.m. The coronation was to begin at 8 p.m.; Susana Zavaleta at 9 p.m. Fireworks were set for 10 p.m.

Rocio, Zacatlan's Queen, was introduced and cheered. Dignitaries had their moment. I drifted away from the speeches, but returned when I heard the band. It was rock and roll. I knew the songs in English, but lyrics were in Spanish. *"Boney Maroney"* in Spanish became as "skinny as a skelton." *"Jailhouse Rock"* had my feet moving. *"Good Golly, Miss Molly,"* *"Lucille,"* could things get better? The answer was "Yes!"

Forty beautiful women dressed in finery and wearing sashes lined up. Each was a queen from her community, association, club or school. There were more queens in Zacatlan than in European history.

The pageantry of the beauty queens was followed by the artistry of Susana Zavaleta, a cabaret singer, comedienne, vamp and performer. She reminded me of Cher with her high black leather boots, black shorts, open midriff, black leather halter, waist-length, black straight hair, torch songs and risqué banter. She was confident, she teased the audience with her quick wit. Then she sang and showed her vocal range. I kept wondering, "This is the Apple Fair?"

127

An hour rolled by. The Palacio Municipal (City Hall) exploded in fireworks. Dazzling, whirling, rocketing fireworks engulfed the block-long facade. The night was lit up; smoke descended like fog.

I thought Bernardo missed the show. But I was wrong. He called to say he had arrived. I walked over to his hotel and brought him back to the plaza. This is Mexico. Parties start at my bedtime. Los Castro (three Castro brothers) took the indoor stage at 11 p.m. The program shifted from song to comedy and back again. It was a brotherly rat pack. I was frustrated. Out of 600 people, I was the guy who didn't get the joke. The humor was quick story telling and one-liners. My Spanish was deficient for the spicy fun.

At 3:45 a.m. the lead singer indicated that it was the last number. The audience chanted, "Otra, otra, otra, otra." The two most enthusiastic chanters were seated at the head table, Mary Carmen and Bernardo. They were clapping and repeating, "Otra, otra, otra." I was the only weary soul in the hall.

Los Castro entertained for another hour. It was wonderful to be back in Las Vegas, back in the '60s. However, I'm in my 60s, too. But so was a good portion of the crowd. Where was my energy? Los Castro continued. Then the comedian brother wound it up, but not before more "Otras."

I was ready to leave, twitchy in my chair. Mary Carmen said, "Now the dance." My weary face caved. She asked incredulously, "Do you want to leave?" I told her that I came to stay to the end, even if I would be carried to the cemetery.

At 5 a.m. it was a salsa band. Mary Carmen and Bernardo danced, moving and shaking. Hardly anyone had left, and most seemed to be on the dance floor. I wouldn't consider getting out of my chair. I thought, "I may be here to the end, but I will be seated." I hadn't been up this late at a dance since my high school prom.

We were one of the first to leave just before 6 a.m. Mary Carmen announced, "Breakfast, 10 a.m., Campestre La Barranca."

I walked back to the hotel, wondering about the cost of this fabulous evening. I started this day at 6:30 a.m., headed for the plaza and the Green Bus. I had set a personal endurance record that will never be broken.

Tomorrow there would be Kwaxochitl and another seven days of entertainment! But that would be for others. Tomorrow I would return to San Luis Potosi and prepare for the second leg of my cross-country trip.

Carterista: Pickpocket or Wear a Money Belt!

I arrived in San Luis Potosi, planned to leave early the next morning and mentally calculated the cash I'd need for hotels, buses and meals. I went to HSBC Bank's ATM, next door to Hotel Plaza Real, punched in my card and code, and loaded my wallet.

Friends, Santiago and his family, expected me for dinner, and I was running late. My plan was to take my host a Selva Negra (Black Forest cake) from a master pastry chef in San Luis Potosi.

I tried to catch the bus near my hotel but I stood on the wrong corner; it was not a bus stop and the bus barreled on by. But good luck, a taxi was right behind. I flagged him down, and said, "Chaires." I was off to buy a Black Forest cake. I didn't realize it then, but the jackpot bars had lined up for a thief: bursting wallet, haste, missed bus, and I hailed the wrong cab.

I got into the taxi and sat in the front seat next to the driver. He zipped straight down Avenida Carranza. It was a short, quick ride. The fare was 17 pesos ($1.60) on the meter. With honest taxi drivers in San Luis Potosi, the meters work, you don't have to bargain.

The taxi stopped in front of Chaires. I brought out a 20-peso note. The driver searched his pockets for change. "Do you have any small change sir?" He was polite. Change is not an unusual problem in Mexico. I had put my wallet back into my front left pocket, and I was sitting down, so it was probably not tucked deep

129

into my pocket.

In the front seat of the taxi I was a little scrunched. I reached with an awkward struggle into my right pocket for change. The taxi driver, keeping up a patter of, "sorry, no change" reached across the steering wheel with his left hand and opened the ashtray to show me there was only a peso and a half for change. He was good-natured and somewhat theatrical and apologetic.

I should have caught the left-hand move, and of course, his right hand was free. I was distracted, ill seated, and reaching for my change, which came to 15 pesos.

He said, "That's okay," and started to give me my 20-peso note. Of course, I was not going to cut the fare down; he was a friendly, courteous driver. I said, "Oh, no, you keep the 20."

I waved good-bye, entered Chaires and ordered a cake. I reached into my vacant pocket and realized, "I was just privileged to witness an Oscar-winning performance of charade and deception."

I lost cash, personal notes and my student registration card from Academia Hispano Americano in San Luis Miguel de Allende, my California Alumni Card, and my ego took a hit. Credit cards and ID were safe in my money belt.

It was a surprise. I wasn't in a crowd where I would have been alert. I was in San Luis Potosi, feeling at home, safe and secure. I wondered, "How often have I been a target when circumstances didn't play into the hands of a thief?"

Often I've stated, "Paranoia is the mother of a safe trip." I forgot my own advice. I dug into my money belt and paid for the Black Forest cake. The Selva Negra cake was delicious. You get what you pay for, and it cost plenty!

DAY 15

Rio Verde, Media Luna, Tamasopo Falls and Puente de Díos: Stage 2

Bus Journey across Mexico

I peeked at my clock. It was 6:14 a.m. There was time to catch the first bus to Rio Verde. It was still dark when my taxi dropped me off at Bus Central. The depot was brightly lit, its counters open, clerks were cheerful, ready to answer questions and sell a ticket.

"Rio Verde," I said. The clerk punched in numbers on the computer keyboard and asked my name, "Ricardo."

It was only two hours and fifteen minutes to Rio Verde, but the world changed. San Luis Potosi is high desert, cactus-loving brown. Rio Verde (Green River) is over the mountains on the gulf side and was humid and wet, and green.

We pulled into Rio Verde, and I bought a taxi ticket in the bus station. Tickets are sold to control the taxi drivers. It protects the passenger from price gouging and the bus station from losing their percentage for the right to pick up passengers. I told the driver, "Downtown."

Rio Verde is a commercial town, but with a very attractive center, a well-kept plaza and attractive church, with a statue of St. Francis.

I checked into Hotel Arcos Vista Bonita. The room was reasonable, $27, but I had to ask for a reading lamp. An attractive restaurant occupied the second floor, with a view of the church and plaza below and scenes of Rio Verde on the walls.

I put my belongings on the bed and went to the plaza, crossed the street to the taxi stand and negotiated. I wanted to see Media Luna and have time to take a few pictures. We agreed on $5 an hour.

Media Luna (Half Moon) is a huge natural spring, crescent shaped, with underwater caves. The water is pure, crystalline, and a near constant ninety-two degrees. The road was dirt, and the taxi driver drove in a serpentine pattern avoiding potholes and ruts.

Jacques Cousteau explored here. An underwater petrified forest, ancient fossils and ten species of fish attracted divers. Clarity of the water was ideal for scuba diving and training.

The road paralleled a canal, which delivered the spring's enormous water flow to farms, ranches and orchards. Oranges, bananas, sugar cane, corn, tomatoes and chilies are crops.

I had seen aerial photos of Media Luna, but I wasn't impressed. Its form seemed a curiosity. But what the photos failed to convey was that Media Luna was also a tree-shaded, camping, picnicking and barbecuing vacation oasis. Children were swimming in a warm river that flowed from the spring. The water was as clear as any I'd ever seen.

On the way back to town I asked Jorge, my driver, to stop near the canal so I could take a picture of what I called a "sun-star" flower, a flower growing among the lily pads, with a yellow center circled by white petals.

As we drove near, two young boys were in the canal cutting the flowers. We stopped. I introduced myself and asked the older boy his name. "Eddie," he said. I took out my Polaroid, snapped Eddie's picture and gave it to him. I took a few digital photos for myself.

Eddie called to his friend, who brought him a plastic Fresca bottle, which had the top cut off. Eddie cut three sun-star flowers, put them in the Fresca vase and offered them to me. "Para la señora (For your wife)," he said.

I thanked Eddie, but on the way back to town, I told the taxi driver, "I'm single, here's for your wife."

The driver laughed. "My wife left me fifteen years ago."

"Well, here's good luck for a new girlfriend," I said. We laughed. We were two old guys with ammunition and no target.

I skipped lunch and caught the next bus to Tamasopo, a place renowned for its waterfalls and cascades. I wasn't disappointed. The falls were a gushing torrent. Rivers and cascades joined to create another vacation paradise. Adam and Eve must have bathed here, and the Tree of Knowledge had to be nearby.

Families and children were enjoying the beach, the sand, wading and swimming. Young men, with no fear of heights, climbed the cliffs and dove into the river as if racing the waterfall to see who would splash first. What a beautiful area!

It was late afternoon. I had taken the bus to the Tamasopo turnoff, but you had to take a taxi from the highway to the falls, about six miles. I negotiated $5 an hour so I could see a variety of cascades. But after a hike to see Puente de Díos (God's Bridge), my stomach was growling. I invited my driver to lunch. "You choose the place," I said. Fernando, my driver, chose a small, modest, family restaurant.

Expenses: Buses $21, taxis: $38, meals: $12, Hotel Arcos: $27. Total: $98

DAY 16
The Mission Corridor to Xilitla

Bus Journey across Mexico

What a day!! It's amazing what a traveler can accomplish in a day, starting early, and using Mexico's efficient bus system and economical taxis.

Father Junipero Serra is esteemed as the Father of California Missions, but he's also venerated in Mexico as the founder of the Sierra Gorda Missions: Concá, Jalpan, Landa de Matamoros, Tilaco and Tancoyol.

Following the arrival of Father Junipero Serra in 1750 in the Sierra Gorda of Central Mexico, five Baroque missions were built using indigenous artists and stonemasons. Each mission façade is a masterpiece and listed as a UNESCO World Heritage Site. Each is unique and reflects the fusion of indigenous and Spanish cultures. The missions are remote. Paved roads to all five were not constructed until 1963.

These missions were neglected until the 1960s when their Baroque façades, with indigenous elements in the iconography, were appreciated. Tilaco, the most elaborate and known as the jewel of the Sierra Gorda Missions, was so remote that a road had to be built before renovating the mission. The first workhorse truck had to be dismantled, carried over the mountains, and reassembled.

I started early, although I hate to roll out of bed before the dawn. When I get up, I want to see sunshine, or at least be aware that the sun is up before me. But dawn comes about 7 a.m. in Rio Verde and that was the hour my bus left the terminal for the Sierra Gorda, a paradise of mountains, gorges, a river and valley towns.

The Rio Verde taxi driver must have felt the same about rising before dawn. There was no cab waiting at the stand to take me to the bus terminal, but I had time to walk the mile or so, about twenty minutes. The clerk remembered my name, Ricardo, and when I asked for a ticket to Concá, she automatically typed in my name and assigned me seat number three, same as the day before, when I went to Tamasopo.

I had five missions to visit, three on the same route, two hidden in the mountains. I figured I could take the bus to three and negotiate with taxi drivers for the side trips to the other two. Yes, buses do trek into the Sierra Gorda, but some routes are daily, not hourly, when you leave the main road, highway 120.

The day went smoothly. I was soaked in the rain, burned in the sun, rode buses and taxis, marveled at the missions, ate breakfast in Concá, met the Secretary of Tourism, took a zillion photos, skipped lunch in favor of Cokes, checked into hotel El Castillo in Xilitla, ate a supper of Pollo a la Mexicana (Chicken Mexican Style), and by 6:30 p.m. I was using the Internet at the Cyber Cafe. That's a lot of activity packed into twelve hours.

The early morning bus driver from Rio Verde believed his passengers had snoozed enough. Before backing out of the stall, he turned on Norteño polka-accordion music. He liked it loud and because he was the driver, he got his choice. We oompahed, oompahed, oompahed, oompahed for the next hour, in and out of three towns. The lyrics were clear. It's not a bad way to practice your Spanish on a trip.

I rummaged through my shoulder bag but found that I had left my notes someplace. I wasn't sure of all the missions' names. I asked the driver, "Is there a mission in Concá?"

"Concá?" he repeated. "There is nothing there. There is an old hacienda."

As we approached Concá, the mission church stood out against the skyline, tall steeple, a tower and a half-dome vault. Sometimes I wonder what I said in Spanish and what I think I said.

I had an hour to see the mission and eat breakfast. There was plenty of time; the town's main eatery was a block from the church. I walked the eight blocks to the small restaurant where a sign read, "Gloria's Restaurant Secretary of Tourism."

Gloria turned out to be a bouncy, four-feet eight-inch charmer and cook. I asked about the Secretary part. She said, "That's for tourists, they come in for advice and find a place to eat."

The tortilla man, with loud, amplified sound coming from his truck, parked in front without turning off the truck's engine or sound system. Gloria and I were talking, but he interrupted. "Business must be good," I thought, "when they bring in tortillas by truck." I thanked her for breakfast and left to see the mission church.

The church was adorned with wonderful iconographic sculptures. I took photos but kept an eye on the time. Then I walked quickly to the terminal. When I reached into my pocket to pay for my ticket, I realized I had stiffed Gloria.

I imagined my bill taped to the cash register for all tourists to see, "This gringo left without paying!" Luckily, a taxi was at hand. I had five minutes. I said to the clerk at the bus counter, "Please don't let the bus leave without me." The taxi driver drove straight to Gloria's. She was smiling. I paid for breakfast and rushed back.

The next two missions, Jalpan and Landa, were easy stops along the way. Tilaco and Tancoyol were somewhat remote but easy taxi rides. They were well worth the economical fare.

The only mission of the five that had any activity was in Jalpan, a city rather than a mountain village, and it was Father Serra's administrative center for the missions. In remote Tilaco, a local taxi driver was playing chess with a friend in the back seat of the cab. While I was chatting with them, two curious young girls came close. I took out my Polaroid, snapped their photos and instantly presented them with a gift.

I was concerned after a final side trip to Tancoyol when the taxi driver left me on a barren stretch of the main highway to catch the next bus, and a rainsquall arrived with raindrops the size of nickels. I tried to find shelter under a tree, but the tree's canopy only broke the large raindrops into smaller ones. Just as I could

feel my Timberline water-repellent jacket no longer repelled and panic was setting in, I spotted two headlights in the rain, hailed the bus and rode in dry comfort to Xilitla. August mornings are grand in Mexico, but afternoon showers can strike quickly with a ferocious, tropical downpour.

I checked into El Castillo, once the private home of Edward James, now a unique bed and breakfast with swimming pool and art treasures. I sat in my room and reviewed the missions in my camera's LED display, read a brochure and organized my experience. I visited the Cyber Café, which was open late.

I took out my notes typed: Sierra Missions, and sent myself the following email.

The bus route followed a corridor of five mission churches, each adorned and painted in folk-churrigueresque Baroque style that glorified the Franciscan Order, incorporating symbols of the knotted cord, stigmata, and the crossed arms of Christ and St. Francis. The church façades were painted, polychromed, in radiant, brilliant colors, decorated with a sculptured profusion of native plants and vines, with niches for saints and ornamented with the doubled-headed eagle, both a Spanish-Hapsburg and indigenous symbol. Each façade was a sermon in stone.

An open-aired atrium enclosed a wide plaza in front of each church where biblical story-dramas accompanied by music and dance were often performed to educate and convert the native population. Iron-forged crosses stood protected by roundabouts in the courtyards, which offered bench seating, and the crosses themselves gave further evidence of the quality of workmanship provided by the indigenous people.

Concá was the smallest yet the most colorful. Its yellow tower stood out against the blue sky. The Holy Trinity crowned the church and St. Michael, sword in hand, placed his foot on the devil. St. Roque stood with his faithful dog. St. Francis and St. Anthony flanked the Moorish-styled entrance. A rabbit, an indigenous symbol, pranced on the sidewall. Original colors, rust, ochre and china blue, had been restored.

A clock occupied the central niche where a statute of St. James once stood in the church at Jalpan, which was also the administrative headquarters for the missions. St. Peter and St. Paul guarded the arched entrance, and the patron saints of Spain and Mexico, the Virgin of Pilar and the Virgin of Guadalupe, were placed above St. Dominic and St. Francis. The double-headed eagle in the lower base looked more Aztec than Hapsburg.

Landa, the last of the missions to be built, was more complex than Jalpan and venerated the Virgin of the Immaculate Conception. It stood brightly painted in deep red and ochre. Two intellectual defenders of the faith, both sitting at their writing desks, Duns Scot and the Blue Nun, were depicted over the entrance.

Tilco, the most remote, was the most elaborate and most cheerful mission. Cherubs and angels, some playing instruments, some smiling with joy, gave one a sense of heaven. St. Joseph, dressed in brightly colored robes, carried the Christ Child, who pulled on his beard. In this quiet village the local taxi driver played chess in the back seat with a friend.

Tancoyol stood out, with its atrium walls decorated with conical "turk's heads" and finials. The color scheme was ochre and pale yellow, but was still brilliant. The Virgin was missing from her niche, and the dominant scene was St. Francis receiving the stigmata from the Divine.

Expenses: Buses: $9, taxis: $27, meals: $12, Hotel El Castillo $60, Total: $108

DAY 17
Xilitla: Edward James, El Castillo and Las Pozas

Bus Journey across Mexico

Sleeping Beauty would have been wide-awake in Edward James' Castle, unless she felt no need for privacy. You are a guest in a home, not a hotel. My first-floor bedroom was designed for flow-through ventilation, with a ceiling fan wafting a pleasant light breeze during the night. Windows opened to the hallways. But as a guest among strangers, I felt the need to close the windows. This interfered with the circulation, and the room became humid and warm.

El Castillo is a pleasure, and the traveler must stay here. Edward James placed his artistic imprint on his home. It is a treasure. Guests are free to wander this multistory fantasy structure and to photograph the inspiring views of Xilitla and the lush terrain, where the principal crop is coffee. There is a swimming pool and a large family reading room that runs the full length of the building. It's currently used as the guests' dining room. An Egyptian-inspired fantasy created by Leonora Carrington accents the doorway, and in the morning the hallway is dappled with sunlight that is scattered by a honeycomb pattern of windows.

A recent addition is the Edward James Museum. There is a photo history of James, but the most interesting items are the hand-carved molds used in the construction of James' surrealistic garden, Las Pozas.

Saturday morning I walked this hill town. Gray mist and humid banks of smoke-like fog enveloped the valley with a

Shangri-La impression of lost time and mystery. Vendors were taking over the plaza and side streets, setting up stalls and canopies to shelter buyers and merchandise. Breakfast in El Castillo was at 8.30 a.m. I felt like James or a member of his family starting a day in Xilitla, casually, with the sun lighting the steep-walled valley dappled with fog.

I came here to see Edward James' Las Pozas, a garden in the jungle, an inspired, surreal fantasy garden constructed of concrete that makes you think of Salvador Dalí in three dimensions. Mexicans call it a "dream catcher."

Las Pozas (The Pools) opened at 9 a.m. I walked the mile downhill from El Castillo to Las Pozas. This magnificent surrealistic garden constructed in the heart of nature's garden attracted young couples, travelers in love. Las Pozas covers acres, and you can see only a glimpse at a time. Workers are constantly cutting back vines and plants. Trails wind up the mountainside, and you hear the waterfalls before you see them. Swimmers enjoy the pool under a large waterfall.

But it was James' imagination that created the trails and ornamental concrete flowers painted in bright colors, the snakes and bridges, archways and oval entrances and multilevel spiral stairways, framed by fantasy columns and concrete bamboo fences. Those are the things make Las Pozas a rich reward for the artist and a pleasure for all visitors.

Among waterfalls and pools, James created thirty-six structures on eighty acres in his private jungle garden. They appear animated by Gaudí's architectural vision and Dalí's dreams. There are Gothic arches, parabolic entryways, and columns erupting into blossoms. James added stairways and bridges that M.C. Escher might have envisioned.

Only in Mexico can one walk through such a fantasy garden within nature's garden. Handrails were nonexistent. Like the Winchester House in San Jose, California, there were stairways to nowhere except the imagination. A spiral staircase led up to an overlook, a platform above an arch six stories high. I crept up, hugging the support column, but vertigo halted me.

I returned to earth safely. I took photos realizing the truth that, "One picture is worth a 1000 words." I walked through Las Pozas, quietly savoring the aesthetic flow like a practitioner of *feng shui* in harmony with *chi.*

At noon I looked at my map for the Corredor de Minas (Corridor of Mines), which, like the corridor of missions, would take me through another remote, steep-valley sierra. Four mining towns were possibly on the agenda, but for most of the day I'd be catching buses and making multiple transfers.

At 12:30 p.m., hot and sweating, I caught an air-conditioned bus for La Y Griega. Step-by-step, bus-by-bus, I connected the dots from town to town in the Sierras. The towns were generally small, roadside commercial centers for farmers and ranchers. At no time did I wait longer than fifteen minutes for a connection. On most routes, Mexico's bus system is efficient and economical. I trusted in luck and had not been disrupted in my travels.

From La Y Griega to Tomechtla to Huejutla to Zacualtipan, I rode in comfort. A young man with a guitar boarded the bus at La Y Griega and played *huapangos* en route to the next stop.

The bus gave me a picture-window view of the Sierra, its jungle, prehistoric flora, ferns, vines, brush and bush, trees, both deciduous and pine, but only a few flowers, maybe due to a predominance of shade. Our route, a narrow road, was cut into steep cliffs. Yet, among this natural beauty, there was subsistence farming and cornfields. Tall green stalks were growing, generally not terraced, on sixty-degree inclines.

In the valleys, along the road, woodworkers displayed their merchandise: chairs, rocking horses, tables, bureaus, dining room sets, coffee tables, all sparkling, polished and varnished to a high luster.

By early evening, I reached the roadside bus stop at Zacualtipan. I took a taxi to town, a large commercial and textile town. I checked into the Palacios Hotel and ate a light supper in their restaurant. There was a party in the hotel. The guest of honor was celebrating his 75th birthday with friends, family and three mariachi bands. As soon as one band left, another arrived. I listened for a while then took a walk to the main square. It was traditional and attractive, but mainly a commercial center.

The next morning I would visit mining towns. There was no need for an alarm clock. The rooster next to my hotel room was the Glen Miller King of Kikirikis (cock-a-doodle-doos). I think the rooster had perfect pitch; his cry was a delight.

Expenses: Buses: $12, taxi: $4, meals: $21, Hotel Palacios $24, Total: $61.

DAY 18
Sierra Gorda: Mining Towns and Pachuca

Bus Journey across Mexico

I woke up too early for breakfast and repeated my walk of last night in Zacualtipan. All was quiet. The streets were vacant, and stalls in the plaza were closed, but I was in two worlds.

There was a world of supermarkets and farmers markets, modern and traditional. Signs advertised patented medicine, and herbs for making a tea for just about anything that ailed you were sold in the plaza. Doctors' clinics offered ultrasound and computer analysis. New homes, broadcasting conspicuous consumption, stood across from corrugated, tin-roofed shacks, which were decorated with flowers in pots that were lovingly cared for.

I caught an 8 a.m. bus. Breakfast would be in Real del Monte, an old mining town. Looking out the bus window, I felt like I was viewing the background for the original King Kong movie. Driving the Sierra Gorda Corridor of Mining Towns, you are surrounded by a sense of the forgotten world, a primeval forest. Peering through the bus window, plants seemed like a picture book of pop-up cutouts.

There were two former mining towns along the main route Zacualtipan-Pachuca that I wanted to visit, Real del Monte, and El Chico, now a biosphere reserve, the oldest in Mexico, established in 1892 by President Porfirio Diaz.

Real del Monte is famous for *pastes* (pronounced pas-tays),

originally a miner's meal of meat and potatoes baked in pastry, like a turnover. *Pastes* are now filled with just about anything, and even those filled with fruit are often called *pastes* instead of turnovers or *empanadas*.

The bus let me off at the roadside. I walked down hill about a half mile to Real del Monte. Real del Monte looked like a Hollywood movie set. Hills

155

formed a backdrop for the town, with arches, plaza and church. Buildings seemed to be harmonized in pastel colors. The premier *paste* restaurant was under the arches. I ordered the traditional *paste* of meat and potatoes and an apple turnover and coffee. I was curious about the *paste;* it was new to me.

The waitress, a friendly woman, showed me the kitchen. There were a number of busy workers; I felt singed by the heat from the ovens. They made empanadas and *pastes* for much of the town, and tourists took them home by the dozens.

I asked about the *paste*. She said, "It came from the English." She showed me how the *empanada* is folded, but the *paste* is creased, pinched along the edge. The *paste* is a real meal. It's filled with potatoes and chili. It's got a bite. She said. "Miners took *pastes* with them for their lunch underground."

I walked outside. Stores opened at 10 a.m. The silver shops and restaurants attracted tourists. There was a mining tour and a double-decked faux English bus for the city tour. The bus was stubby-short so the driver could navigate the steep hills and tight corners.

I brought out my camera, but the place was under siege. Photographers were everywhere, pointing cameras and setting up tripods. I looked through my lens; photographers were like polka dots. They were in every possible scene. It was a student class from Mexico City, and they'd rightly chosen Real del Monte as a picturesque mountain town.

Real del Monte has a history of mining; the first mining strike in the Americas took place here. It's a beautiful mountain setting, and much wealth was spent on architecture. I noted a touch of English presence. English mining engineers put English roofs on Spanish buildings for ventilation and protection from the rain. Most roofs were corrugated sheet metal, and someone decided that they should be painted red. Red roofs, steep, winding streets, a church tower influenced by London's Big Ben, plazas, arcades, portals, all combined to stimulate the artist and photographer.

I tried to take a few pictures of the town without the student photographers and their tripods, when I saw an open-sided tour bus, looking like a San Francisco cable car. It offered a forty-minute tour, with guide and commentary, for 25 pesos ($2.25).

It gave a great view of the city from the English cemetery and a brief history. The guide claimed that Real del Monte was the city with the highest elevation in Mexico. He said we were 2800 meters high, over 8000 feet. But his best information was that the last working mine, the La Mina Rica, closed on January 14, 2005, and now offered a tour. We could descend in a miners' cage 1300 feet, deeper than the Empire State Building is tall, and see the inside of a mine. I followed directions and got to the La Mina Rica. There was already a good-sized group waiting. I signed up, and they honored my Berkeley student ID (I take Senior Classes).

I got into blue overalls, put on a yellow safety helmet with a miner's light attached to the front and a cord leading to a battery pack held on a leather belt around the overalls. I was ready. We took turns getting into the miners' elevator, a double-decked arrangement. Our guide pulled the flex-gate closed, rang a bell-signaling system, and one cable dropped us 1300 feet straight down. We zipped past rock walls broken in places by tunnels. We felt the cool air and the pressure change. It was smooth and swift and stopped perfectly at the bottom platform.

We gathered together and were told not to raise our hands because there were live electric cables overhead, and not too far overhead either, I noticed. The guide said, "We will be walking through an access tunnel, then we'll get on a miners' trolley and drive over a mile deep to the face of the mine." We would see the vein that the miners followed for years, but which finally became unproductive. At the current price of silver, it was not profitable to continue.

We walked and took pictures. We saw abandoned ore carts, rusted iron supports, hard-rock tunnels branching off and narrow tracks. We stopped and looked into an even deeper pit. The guide silenced us, and we listened to a rock fall 150 feet. We listened to it bounce off the walls of the shaft and heard the rockslides and sifting dirt that followed.

The guide took us to the face and pointed out the vein. We all got our chance to rub the vein for luck. Then in an open area, we formed a circle and stopped. No one moved, and we all turned out our miner's light. In the depth of the mine, it was pitch black. Nothing registered. It was pure absence of visual sensation.

The guide said that anyone could speak and offer reflections.

"You're anonymous," he said. One woman spoke up. She said that her father had worked in this mine for fourteen years, and this was the first time she had been in a mine. The thought of his labor here stirred her feelings. She felt a connection, a respect and reverence.

Another spoke in the darkness. He reflected on the value of sight and how blessed we were, not only for sight but for the fact that we were healthy and could visit a mine. The mood turned more reflective and spiritual. It was like a religious camp moment, giving thanks and witness to the grace of God.

El Chico, the second town, with a history of silver mining, was a taxicab drive into the pine forest, which President Diaz was wise to set aside. This ecological preserve attracts family vacationers. The town is a small gem, only a few blocks in size, located on a mountain slope.

From El Chico I caught the collective taxi for Pachuca, the capital of the State of Hidalgo. Pachuca is a large city with a touch of colonial architecture. The collective let me off a few blocks from the city center and the symbol of Pachuca, a towering monumental clock, which was made by the same manufacturer as London's Big Ben in the late 1800s.

Near the clock and bell tower, a woman, shaded by sitting under a red-blue-yellow umbrella, was selling city tours. The man in front of me bought the last four tickets. I told the lady who had just sold the last ticket, "I'd like to take this tour, and I'm willing to stand."

She called to Laura, the tour guide, "Do you have room for one more?" Laura asked me, "Would you mind sitting up front with me?" I saw Pachuca in an hour. I don't think I missed a thing.

Tlaxcala, the city that allied with Cortes to defeat the Aztecs, was next on my agenda.

Expenses: Bus and shared taxis: $15, meals: $9, Hotel $30, City Tour: Pachuca $4. Total: $58.

DAY 19
Tlaxcala: Faithful Allies to Cortes

Bus Journey across Mexico

History books imply that Cortes, with a small Spanish army, defeated the Aztecs because of superior armor, horses, guns and the belief that Cortes was the returning god, Quetzalcoatl. The question of "deity" was quickly dismissed. He had sixteen horses, two of which were killed in the first battle, and he led an army of 400 men. He conquered Mexico City, a city of a quarter million people, and dominated a land inhabited by over fifteen million people. It was his strategic alliance with the Tlaxcala Indians and other tribes that enabled Cortes to proceed and conquer. Thousands of Tlaxcalans supported Cortes against the Aztecs and wept when he returned to Spain.

If it were not for Tlaxcalans, the conquistador of Mexico might have not have been named Cortes. Tlaxcalans allied with Cortes against the Aztecs. The Tlaxcalans were the most important, loyal and faithful allies of the Spanish. I doubt that without their

warriors, and the bearers of logistics, Cortes could have vanquished the Aztecs in 1521.

I wanted to observe this land where Cortes fought and won the loyalty of the Tlaxcalans, and see their history told in the famous mural painted on the Palacio Municipal's walls.

Tlaxcala is the oldest colonial town in Mexico. The government seat was founded in 1524. It is

HERNAN CORTES DE MONROY

163

considered the Cradle of a New Race, the *mestizo*, the union of the Spanish with the indigenous.

The morning air was refreshing, and Tlaxcala was a short, winding ride from Pachuca. I arrived a little after 9 a.m. The bus driver let me off on the outskirts and pointed out where to catch a collective taxi, a *combi*. I scarcely got off the bus and blinked when the *combi* picked me up. Within minutes I was in the center of Tlaxcala at the tourist information booth.

I stayed at Hotel Posada San Francisco on the main square. It was once a private mansion in the 19th century. The building has been lovingly restored. It's the place to stay, with a fine restaurant, an inner patio, a bar decorated in grand style, and a beautiful, clean, inviting pool, which were just a few feet from my room.

Tlaxcala remains a colonial jewel in the mountains. A fountain, which was donated by a Spanish king, is the focal point in its plaza. Unlike many Mexican plazas surrounded by arched portals, outdoor dining is encouraged. I was pleased to see two coffee shops; I often wish for a casual place to sit and contemplate when in Mexico and find very few.

I picked up a city map. There were twenty-two sites, museums, churches, and

164

historic buildings. Most of the interesting places in a colonial town are near the original center, so tourists with maps in hand, can walk and visit at their own pace. During the day I visited eighteen of the twenty-two sites.

I pushed on the door of the Museum of Memory. The door was open but the museum, I was quickly told, was closed. Of the four museums, only Tlaxcala's regional museum was open.

Walking the streets of Tlaxcala, I followed the paths of history. Vivid murals in radiantly vibrant colors by the artist Desiderio Hernandez Xochitiotzin outlined Tlaxcala's history in the Palacio Municipal. In my mind they were equal to any of Diego Rivera's. I huffed and puffed my way uphill to the Santuario de Ocotlán, a

165

spectacular wedding-cake-white, Baroque church honoring the Virgin. It has been the site of pilgrimage since 1541 when the Virgin appeared here. And I stopped at the Capilla de Pocito de Agua (Chapel of the Small Well) where the water is considered sacred and miraculous.

The Antigua Casa de Piedra (Ancient House of Stone), once a private mansion, is now Hotel San Francisco, a fine luxury hotel. The Capilla de San Francisco (Chapel of St. Francis), part of one of the earliest monasteries, housed the original stone baptismal basin where four Tlaxcalan chiefs were baptized upon conversion to Christianity. Tlaxcala honors the four chiefs and also Xicotencatl, a recalcitrant foe who tried to rouse his people against the Spaniards.

Outside the city are two magnificent archaeological sites, which were only excavated in 1975. Cacaxtla is a unique temple complex with vibrant, preserved frescos of the battle between Birdmen and Jaguarmen. Nearby lies the less complex but larger ruin of Xochitecatl with both a standard large pyramid and a spiral mound.

Next stop: Puebla, the City of Tiles. Less than two hours away, Puebla was only a $5 bus ride from Tlaxcala.

Expenses: Bus and taxis $6, meals $30, Hotel San Francisco $75, laundry $7, Total: $116.

DAY 20
Puebla and Popotillo

Bus Journey across Mexico

Puebla is the Talavera jewel of Mexico. If one could slice Puebla's colonial center into a baker's dozen, the result would be twelve additional world-class, eye-catching architectural beauties: Brick and Talavera, facades of Alfenique, rich Baroque designs, Moorish and Andalusian. Even the neglected emanate a beauty that stops the traveler and demands reflection.

Changing sunlight sets off and highlights marvelous intricate designs reflecting from the Talavera tiles and creates contrasts with the matte brickwork. Moving shadows fashioned by drifting clouds break the sunlight into patterns, making scenes fresh, like twirling a kaleidoscope prism.

It always strikes me as ironic that what is truly beautiful in Mexico is mixed with a legacy of controversy: the Spanish dons, the Catholic clergy and Porfirio Diaz.

Puebla, Mexico's fourth largest city claims to have been inspired by angels. Truly, Puebla abounds with architectural masterpieces, and beauty is so commonplace it's taken for granted by those who live here. It's an outdoor art show. I stare, look up and around, and I seem to be alone in my

astonishment. The map tells me there are over 1200 colonial and architecturally splendid buildings, tiled and decorated, located in the center of Puebla. Pedestrians look straight ahead and go about their business. But my senses were dazzled.

Puebla is the home of *mole*, the tasty specialty at Fonda de Santa Clara, and the China Poblana, the traditional outfit Mexican waitresses often wear. *Mole* (sauce) is a concoction of chocolate and chili, spicy not sweet. It's a brown sauce generally served on turkey or chicken, and it is considered Mexico's national dish. The China Poblana, the scooped neck, bare-shouldered blouse, with a flouncy skirt, is the national costume, counterpart in Mexican films to the silver-spangled charro outfit.

Puebla's colonial center, founded in 1531, designed and built on a grid, is flat and easy on the legs, ideal for walking. It has the flavor of a European city. I favor lounging under the arches, reading a newspaper, sipping coffee, and enjoying the view of the plaza. I listen to the bullhorn demonstrators protesting a grievance at the Volkswagen plant, yet I come away with the feeling that Puebla is a city of tranquility.

Across from my strangely named hotel, City Express,

170

is one of the oldest neighborhoods in Puebla, this most Spanish of all cities in Mexico. The once elegant neighborhood is now in a state of general decline and advancing barbed wire security precautions. Old houses reflect an age of Gatsby Baroque and conspicuous display. I felt compelled, as if inspecting tombstones in a cemetery, to walk through the neighborhood just to view the decaying splendor.

I took a photo of a Moorish-influenced styled mansion, a bright yellow building with multiple domes encrusted with tiles and pictures in ceramic, scenes from Don Quixote, which decorated the sweeping veranda that took up an entire block. The mansion was for rent. Then I noticed another eye-catching building.

I crossed the street and stood, looking at a fantasy, a pink and red brick castle with a tall, slender, hexagon turret that was balanced architecturally on the opposite side by a short, squat tower with a tiled dome. It had Moorish arched windows and a crenellated roof. I was getting ready to photograph this fantastic home when a tall, slightly built man stepped out from under the arch of the doorway.

I said, "Buenos días."

He answered in English, "Good afternoon." I commented on the beauty of the building and he said, "Step inside; it's cooler."

Inside was a piano, bar, art gallery. My host was Maher Naamanni, a Canadian.

"Pronounce it 'New Money,'" he said.

We sat in the cool bar. I gazed at the art, large paintings along the wall. He said his favorite was *The Carnival,* a rich red modern art painting of a dancing, swirling woman by Magalé. "It's a tragedy," he said, and then explained that Magalé underwent an operation last year and a nerve was severed. "Left him paralyzed from the chest down."

There were five Magalé paintings on the wall. Each was painted in oil, in a different style. It was an impressive collection.

I asked, "What brought you to Mexico?"

"An airplane," he said.

I guessed that he was tired of the question, and I laughed. "Naw, naw," I said, "what motivated you?"

"My father-in-law died." And then he told me his story.

Maher had been working for years, building up a business, putting all his time into making it a success. "When my father-in-law died in 1988, he had five children. They loved him, but within two weeks everything he had … everything, his car, his clothes, furniture … everything was sold and the cash divided. It was as if he had never lived. Right then I wanted to sell my business and do things that I liked. Six months later, I sold."

We talked of his experiences. "What do you like most about Mexico?" I asked

"Every day the sun comes up. Every morning, the same sun. In Montreal, it's pull back the shade and ask, 'What's the weather like?' Here you know, in the morning it's sun."

He told me, "Mexico adapts to people. Everywhere you have to adapt to the country. But here, it's the other way around. And it's family. If your daughter marries and you need another room, you build it, you add on, no permit. If you lose your job, you open a business, put a stand in front of your house. No one complains. The pace is slower." He mentioned that new products traveled slower. "In Montreal, a new gadget comes out, next day, it's cheaper in Vancouver. Here, you can buy leather goods in Leon, truck them to Veracruz and make a profit." Maher hadn't lost his business interest.

"What don't you like?"

"Appointments. I can't tell you how many appointments I've had, and the people don't show up. And loans. If you lend money, people think you've got a lot and they feel as if you don't need to get it back."

A Personal Quest

Years ago I purchased a "painting" made of broom straw in Guanajuato. I call it a painting because that's what it looks like, but up close you see that it's really a mosaic of colored, dyed straw. The artist said, "I'm from Puebla. It's a family tradition and we're about the only artists to use dyed broom straw."

So here I am in Puebla trying to explain the artwork I'm looking for and I get blank stares. I'm fumbling in Spanish. I explain simply, but people think I'm interested in a broom or straw. I just confuse people.

I speak with Ruben Ibarra, the afternoon clerk at the hotel, and I ask him, "Is there a family in Puebla, artists who use broom straw? I'd like to find them."

"You mean *popodillo*?" he asks. "There's a lady who makes them at the Casa del Artesano. And there is a shop." He starts to flip through the telephone directory. Shortly, he's on the phone, telling me that Mary Capilla is the artist at Casa del Artesano but it's after 6 p.m. and she's gone home. Next, he's talking to Amabilia

Meneses who owns a small store. She sells *popodillo*, embroidered dresses, costume jewelry, wooden toys, folk art and a variety of handmade items. Her shop is closed. She's at home now, but she tells Ruben that she'd be happy to show us her merchandise if we would like to come to her house.

Ruben called for a taxi and gave the driver a note with her complete address. The taxi took me into the backside of Puebla. Amabilia lived in a crowded working section of town. The taxi driver found the neighborhood and the street but couldn't locate the address or the building. He stopped and asked. He was directed north into a dead-end street. It was great to know I'm not the only one who gets lost in Mexico.

We turned around and asked again. We were pointed in the right direction but we couldn't find a single number. The driver stopped at a small grocery and asked. The grocer pointed to a cluster of buildings. We were close but still lost. Nearby, teenagers were playing basketball. The driver stopped again and asked. One of the boys ran ahead and pointed toward our destination.

As the taxi rolled to a halt, Amabilia opened her door. She lived up to her name, "Amiable." She was short and wore one of the embroidered dresses that her shop sold. Wooden toys, bobble-headed, bobble-winged turkeys, a variety of children's brightly embroidered dresses, charm bracelets, and at least a dozen soft dolls looking like Raggedy Ann, with straw blond hair were arranged on chairs, a coffee table, and the sofa. The dolls were the only blonds in Puebla. But there were no *popodillos*, and that's what I had come for.

Amabilia said that she had a couple *popodillos* in her shop, but she wanted to show us all her merchandise and maybe we'd like something. She then gave me a bobble-headed, bobble-winged turkey.

Of course one cannot accept a gift in these circumstances without making a purchase. So as I unwrapped my gifts when I arrived home, there were two soft dolls with blond hair made in Mexico for my granddaughters. And on my shelf I placed a treasure, a bobble-headed, bobble-winged turkey. It had somehow become precious.

Mexican Pride: Cinco de Mayo

When I went to San Luis Potosí, Mexico, to teach English, I was surprised to find that May 5 was not a national holiday. It was a major event in Puebla but was scarcely celebrated in San Luis Potosi. It's a big fiesta in the U.S., and I assumed it was celebrated all over Mexico. In fact, a lot of gringos think May 5 is Mexico's Independence Day. Here's one part of the story.

May 5, 1862: The Mexican forces at Puebla defeated the superior

invading French army. This was the first time since Mexico's independence in 1821 that Mexicans won a victory over a European army. It was a source of pride. But it was the beginning battle, not the final victory. It still took five years to expel the French.

Ignacio Zaragosa, named for San Ignacio, the founder of the Jesuit Order, was the victorious general at Puebla. General Zaragosa was born in 1829 in Goliad, Texas, while it was still part of Mexico.

In 1836, Texas became independent from Mexico, and the Zaragosa family was forced to relocate to Matamoros and later to Monterrey, Mexico. So, although General Zaragosa was born Mexican, his birthplace ended up on the U.S. side of the border. After his glorious success over the French, he died of typhus in September 1862.

In 1867, Cinco de Mayo began in Texas as a source of cultural pride. On May 5, 1867, in San Ignacio, Texas, they first celebrated General Ignacio Zaragosa's victory, and other border towns picked up the tradition.

Corridos, Mexican ballads, which are the newspapers and editorials of events, carried the story of the defeat of the French and sang the praises of the Hero of Puebla, the "unconquerable general of the border."

Music, migration and Texas-Mexican pride spread the tradition.

Expenses: Bus-Taxi: $6, Hotel City Express $60, meals $18. Total: $84.

I took a break to be with my family for Thanksgiving then returned in December for the final leg of this adventure, which would take me from Puebla to Chetumal, then up the coast to Tulum and a return flight home from Cancun.

DAY 21
Córdoba: Dancing in the Plaza

Bus Journey across Mexico

I hopped on an ADO (Autobuses de Oriente) bus, First Class, which roared out of Puebla's CAPU Station in pleasant weather and drove southeast into mountain fog, mist and drizzle. I sat next to Maria de los Angeles and chatted all the way to Córdoba. Maria had worked in Las Vegas where she "watched Asians bet $100 chips as if they were grains of rice."

I relaxed and expected a four-hour-plus bus ride through winding mountains from Puebla to Córdoba, which was founded as a military outpost to protect the highway, merchants and travelers from marauders. I looked out the window over deep, lush, green valleys and wondered how apprehensive or confident the Spanish conquistadors felt marching in this mountainous New World. They must have believed in destiny, determination and in rewards to tackle this terrain. The bus zipped into Córdoba in only two hours. I laughed at myself thinking, "Mexico is building highways, tunnels and bridges faster than I'm updating maps."

This modern highway avoided the old wrenching, curving four-hour tummy turner. From my passenger-side window, the looming Orizaba Mountain was profiled against a blue-purple sky, with its perfect peak capped in white looking like a 17,000-foot snow cone. Then fog engulfed us and Orizaba disappeared.

I bought a taxi voucher from the machine at the bus terminal, took the next cab from a waiting row and asked the driver to take me to Córdoba's center. I asked about hotels near the plaza. The driver grunted and then suggested Hotel Bello. "It's a businessman's hotel," he said dryly.

"What's the main industry in Córdoba?" I asked.

The taxi driver said, "Coffee and sugar cane." He didn't elaborate. Our conversation went dead.

Hotel Bello charged $41 a night, offered free Internet in the lobby for guests and an attractive restaurant with large picture windows that flooded the dining area with light. Maplewood straight-backed chairs were set around tables draped with blue tablecloths. The hotel was modern, and the hallway to my room smelled freshly painted, but the shower pressure was low and the water lukewarm.

From the balcony I heard distant music. The plaza was a block away. The Municipal Band was setting up. Workers snapped open folding chairs and set them in rows in the colonial plaza in front of the fountain, across from the Municipal (City Hall). Chairs were shuffled and chrome music stands were unfolded and arranged. Musicians were tuning their instruments, sounding disharmoniously. The band played every Thursday from 6 to 8 p.m.. Tonight was *danzón*, a rhythmic, formal dance, a fusion of African and European influences, which fit the colonial setting.

The maestro waved his baton, the band went silent, then with a stroke the band played and dancers brought their partners forward. It seemed more like Hemingway's romantic Cuba than Mexico. Elders danced and the young watched. I asked a couple, "Why aren't young people dancing?" He answered, "It's difficult. A routine must be followed." Elderly couples were out in force, and ladies were dressed in Sunday elegance, with smart dancing shoes.

I took photos of a lively elderly couple, she in silver shoes, he dressed in white and wearing a white Panama hat. Immediately I took my camera across the plaza to the Fujiphoto. I asked the clerk if they could rush a job. She turned and called, "Fernando." Fernando was working at a computer console. He took my camera chip, told me to come around the counter, inserted the chip into the printer and asked me to point out the pictures on the computer screen. He centered the couple, cropped the photos then zapped the pictures for $2. I walked back to the plaza. When the band took a break, I presented the gift to the surprised couple and told them I enjoyed watching. They graciously accepted the pictures and showed them to their family.

Light showers threatened. With the first drops of rain, the band members gathered their instruments, music stands and chairs and looking like a retreating army, moved under the City Hall archway, the *portales*, which ran the entire length of the building. Once rearranged, the dancing continued until 8 p.m.

The rain stopped. I found a table under the *portales* and ordered dinner. Two mariachis walked by in green charro outfits, short tight embroidered jackets with filigree and silvered spangled trousers. I asked where they were playing. "Right here, at your request." I asked the price and he said, "150 pesos per song."

I thought, "Good price, I can afford a dozen songs." So I lined him up with eleven songs, wrote them down on a napkin and figured 1650 pesos. The two mariachis walked off to gather the rest of the band and a female singer. Two trumpets, three violins, two guitars, a guitarrón (an oversized guitar that plays base), and a singer returned and surrounded my table. My brain started to recalculate,

"That's a large group for the price." Then it struck me. I was thinking $1.50 per song. I had accepted an offer of $15 per song, and they would be expecting $165.

181

I said, "Let me check my wallet." I was embarrassed and told him we'd have to stop at $100 or I wouldn't be able to pay for supper. He offered to play seven songs, giving me a small discount. With all the time I spend in Mexico, you wouldn't think I'd drop a decimal in the exchange rate. I wondered how loudly my old clients would laugh, enjoying the irony of a retired financial adviser who couldn't correctly convert pesos to dollars.

The band started off with "La Negra" (The Black Lady), the mariachis' traditional opening song, worked down my list and ended with "El Rey" (The King), a song about a man who is free and independent, is in essence a king. I enjoyed the music, but the diners under the *portales* didn't seem to care about ballads. This was *danzón* music country.

I chose to sit at a table in front of the historic Hotel Zavavello, which was one reason I wanted to visit Córdoba. After paying the mariachis, I wandered around the old hotel, which was built in 1697. Tiles decorated the walls, and archways led to a patio that once corralled a traveler's horses. It seemed to have changed little in over 300 years. Here in 1821, Don Juan O'Donoju, Viceroy of Spain, after eleven years of war, signed the final accord with Mexico's General Don Agustin Iturbide, which acknowledged Mexico's independence. The two men sealed the pact by going to church, and after mass, returning to Hotel Zavavello, O'Donoju said, "I believe it will be an easy

thing to untie the knot without breaking the connection."

In the morning I grabbed a taxi for the small town called San Lorenzo de Yanga, which is only a short drive from Córdoba. Orizaba, Mexico's highest mountain loomed above as the taxi drove from Córdoba to San Lorenzo de Yanga, or simply Yanga. "De Yanga" was added to the original name San Lorenzo, when Mexico commemorated Yanga, a hero, by adding the brave man's name to his town.

My interest in Yanga began when I was once in Veracruz, visiting an art show titled "The Art of Liberty." I had never thought of Mexican slavery before. The exhibit told the story of Yanga, the Black Prince, a Dinka from West Africa. The art was in panels, telling a story, picture by picture. Paintings depicted Yanga being captured, enslaved and brought to Veracruz in 1570, then in rebellion, leading insurgents and finally breaking the chains of bondage. Yanga led a revolt and escaped with a band of slaves into the mountains of Veracruz where they harassed merchants and travelers and fought a guerilla war against the Spanish militia for over thirty years.

Yanga and his men joined with Indians and white outcasts, begat another generation and were never defeated. The Spanish built the city of Córdoba in an effort to secure the road from Mexico City to Veracruz through the mountains, and still Yanga was a thorn, a rebel and free. The Spanish cursed Yanga as a "cimarrón," an indomitable horse. The solution was liberty, a negotiated peace in 1609 that is the foundation for the town's claim as, "The first free city in the New World."

The taxi parked just off the main plaza, and I walked toward the portales, the adjacent archway, looking for anyone who might give me

183

information. "There won't be a tourist office in this small town," I thought, "I'll ask where the museum is." I assumed that Yanga, a historic town, would have a museum.

Under the archway across from the plaza I met Omar Escalona, Police Comandante. Racially, he was a descendent of Yanga. I asked, "Where is the museum?"

"It won't be open until late August, but I can introduce you to Daniel Cid," the Comandante said.

I didn't know who Daniel Cid was or why I suddenly would be introduced. I'd leave that for later, but for the present I said, "I'd like to know more about Yanga."

"That I can help you with," said the Comandante. "Come to my office."

Within minutes of arriving in Yanga, I was in the police office with Omar Escalona and his personal collection of books and articles on the history of Yanga. "Liberty began here," the police officer said with dignity and authority. I thought it ironic that the man, who represented restriction to many of us, spoke with such pride and confidence in basic rights. Omar Escalona was a comandante imbued with history and ethics.

I asked questions and took notes. Comandante Escalona answered most questions right away but when he wanted to be exact, he opened a book "*Mis Recuerdos: Historia de Yanga*" (My Recollections: History of Yanga) and read aloud. I asked if I could

184

make copies of some of the pages. The comandante lent me his book and said, "There is a shop at the end of the archway. They make copies."

I was still confused about Daniel Cid. "You mentioned Daniel Cid?" I said.

"Oh, yes, I'll have one of my men take you."
Daniel Cid, a self-trained archeologist who lived at the edge of Yanga at a place called Palmillas. His home was the site of his first dig. He donated 8,000 Olmec artifacts to Yanga, and the town had just built a new museum to display the collection. Comandante assumed that I had come to Yanga to interview Daniel Cid and see the new museum.

While pages were being copied, I crossed the street to the plaza. An ornate, octagon-sided, two-story bandstand that was decorated with iron lace, like you see in New Orleans, stood in the center. Rockets boomed, announcing a fiesta. Opposite the bandstand, girls in white dresses and veils and boys in white shirts milled about in front of the church.

I had stumbled into a celebration of a First Communion. Parents were seated in the church. An offering table was set up in the aisle with a fresh basket of fruit, and sprays of roses decorated the church benches. Behind the altar hung a huge cross bearing a crucified Christ, three times taller than the priest. Two banners framed the cross and proclaimed, "I am the bread of life....he that eats of this bread will have everlasting life." The children marched in pairs down the

185

aisle and sat in the first pews. A bell rang, the priest performed the Catholic mass, gave a short sermon then one by one the children received their first communion. They seemed to represent all races, and I noticed a young girl with a radiant first communion smile. She could have been Yanga's daughter.

When I returned, Jaime Gordillo Flores, a businessman, shop owner and father of four, explained that his older daughter designed a symbolic dress for the annual mid-August Yanga carnival, and she won first prize. "Would you like to see the costume?" he asked.

Now we had a real group. Comandante Omar Escalona called in Xavier, a bilingual policeman, to take me to Daniel Cid's. But with Señor Gordillo's offer, we now had two destinations. I wanted to see the monument to Yanga that was built near a local school.

Xavier and I were to follow Jaime's pickup. Xavier was a big guy and the car sagged as he got in and pulled the door shut. He said that he had been on the force for two years but was thinking about opening an English language school. He spoke with hardly a trace of an accent. I asked, "Where in the U.S. did you learn English?"

"I've never been to the U.S.," he said.

I was surprised. He said that he grew up in Córdoba and learned English at a local school.

Xavier asked me what music I liked in Mexico.

I mentioned *"Hombres Malvados"* (Evil Men).

"You like Paquita del Barrio!" Xavier burst out laughing. "I can't believe it. How did you get to know about Paquita?"

I told him. "At home I watch channel 14. I catch the mariachis on the TV."

Xavier grinned and laughed. He felt great joy riding with an American who enjoyed Paquita del Barrio belting out anti-macho lyrics. She has a repertoire of songs that poke fun at pretentious swaggering males and other songs that condemn men for the heartbreak they caused by chasing skirts and losing the women who loved them.

We pulled up behind Jaime's truck. He lived in a modest attractive house with his wife and youngest daughter. His son Jaime was twenty-six, an engineer who worked in Puebla. The older two daughters were in college. Alma, the youngest, was in high school.

Jaime introduced us to his wife Loli, a nickname for Dolores. Loli brought out the prize-winning Yanga dress. On the patio, Jaime started setting up the paintings that they owned that showed their pride in the history of Yanga. I took notes.

I asked if someone could wear the colorful Yanga dress. I thought Alma might volunteer, but immediately Señora Loli said that she would be pleased to put on the dress. She came out wearing a bright orange and green dress embroidered with coffee trees, a variety of fruits and symbols of Yanga. She wore a kerchief and a white blouse accented with orange shoulders. Loli said, "My grandmother was black. When I die, I want drums at my funeral. I'm white on the outside, but black on the inside." Jaime, Loli and Alma stepped on to the patio. I snapped a photo.

Jaime and Loli offered to direct us to the new museum and visit Daniel Cid. "He's over ninety and has been honored by INAH

(National Institute of Archeology and History)." Jaime and Loli drove the pickup and Xavier and I followed.

We parked in front of the nearly complete museum, an attractive white building built around an inner court. It will display Daniel Cid's collection and there will be a separate room for the special history of Yanga.

From the museum it was a short drive to the house of Cid, who lived in a cinderblock house with his wife. Daniel Cid was eager to talk, and when he found out that I spoke Spanish he moved his chair away from Xavier and carried the conversation directly to me. When you're ninety, you get to be in charge. But, I think Señor Cid has always been in charge.

I felt awkward but Xavier was amused. Daniel Cid pulled out volumes of books, which showed artifacts and photos of where he had collected them. I asked, "How did you get started?"

Señor Cid said, "I was in many businesses. I had a truck and this farm. I raised a little corn and as I was plowing, I turned up stones. They were part of a temple pyramid." This pyramid, a small hill today, overgrown with grass, bushes, cactus and even a dying tree, was a short walking distance from his home.

Daniel Cid was enjoying himself, recounting his history, knowing that he had made major contributions. "I've been a member of INAH nearly from the beginning. They started sixty years ago, and I'm been a member for fifty-four years." He must be the longest living member. He said with joy, "When I got old, they honored me. Governor Miguel Aleman and I went to Mexico City, and we

had a great banquet. They felt that I deserved a pension. I had supported myself all those years. They treated me like a general, but they paid me like a recruit." He laughed. He had told this story many times, and he loved having a new audience.

"Can we see the pyramid, the first excavation?" I asked.

"Oh, yes, you can see it," and he went to get more photos. He showed us pictures of a younger self, age 36, slender wearing a white straw fedora, standing in front of an exposed tiered temple, with the unexcavated hill forming the back and sides. "An earthquake caused a landslide and it's a mound of earth now."

He took us to see shelves of some of the minor items and souvenirs from his digs. He had a number of rusty pistols, revolvers and rifles that he had uncovered. I thought, "These weapons have tales to tell."

Xavier was doing very little translating. There just wasn't time, and I followed the conversation with little difficulty. Daniel Cid had the stage, and he enjoyed every moment. He told us about finding gold and how his house became a jail, pointing to the bars on his windows. "Thieves thought I would keep the treasure in my home," he said. "How foolish. They came but the gold was in the bank vault."

We went outside. Daniel Cid and his wife said goodbye and directed us down the dirt country road to the pyramid. I thanked him and said, "Forty years ago I studied in Spain; I know Spain has a Cid. Now I know a Mexican Cid. And I know who is the greater hero."

Xavier, Jaime, his wife Loli and I walked down the dirt road, and if we hadn't been

189

told, we would not have guessed that the nearby hill had been an archeologist's treasure chest. We climbed the pyramid, searched for telltale signs of supporting walls, which were not easy to find. When we stood on top, we could see that there was a second pyramid not far away.

We returned to our cars and headed for the Yanga Monument. The monument was a simple pedestal with a bronze statute sculptured by Erasmo Vázquez Lendechy of a defiant Yanga holding a stalk of sugar cane in his left hand, which had broken the chain of slavery. Raised in his right hand, the machete once used to cut the cane was now his sword of freedom.

It was hot and humid. A dog rested quietly near my car, panting, his eyes and tail moved. Xavier's white shirt showed patches of sweat. We were drained. "Let me buy the refreshments," I offered. Xavier drove back towards town, and then pulled over at a roadside stand with a thatched palm roof. Gravel crunched under the tires as he stopped. The glass-fronted refrigerator was stocked with sodas. I grabbed a twelve-ounce can of Delaware Punch, a noncarbonated grape drink, easy to find in Mexico, hard to find in the U.S. Xavier reached into the upright refrigerator and grabbed a two and one-half-liter (eighty-five ounces) plastic bottle of Sprite. I drank the Delaware Punch and Xavier put away the entire bottle of Sprite, which equaled seven cans of Delaware Punch. I was astonished. It was fitting. It had been an amazing day.

Expenses: Bus $14, taxis $22, meals $28, mariachis $100, Hotel Bello $41. Total: $185.

DAY 22
Coatzacoalcos

Bus Journey across Mexico

I was weary when the ADO bus pulled into Coatzacoalcos. I had traded an intermittent, light drizzle in Córdoba for a tropical downpour in Coatzacoalcos.

In Córdoba I had lingered, walking and sightseeing, and admiring the Christmas decorations. Poinsettias set out in flowerpots lined the plaza and wrapped Córdoba in red. Municipal employees milled around the plaza, chatting in small groups and wearing red uniform jackets as if they were human imitations of the poinsettias in the park.

My leisurely visit cost me. When I went to the bus station and looked at the departure schedule I said, out loud to myself in English, "Bad luck". The clerk smiled. I had forgotten to check the departure schedule for Coatzacoalcos when I arrived, and I missed the bus by five minutes.

Most routes offer frequent service, and rarely am I concerned about departure times, but today five minutes cost me a two-hour wait. I told the clerk I'd take the next bus. She checked the schedule and said, "I'd recommend that you take the 2:40 p.m. ADO bus. It leaves a half hour later, but it's nearly direct, only one stop, and you'll arrive an hour earlier."

I've found the clerks at the central terminals to be constantly alert and helpful. This clerk took thoughtfulness one-step further, "Leave later, and arrive earlier," sounded good to me.

It also proved that travelers should always bring an entertaining thick book for the trip. I had purchased Charles C. Mann's best selling *1491, A History of the Americas Before Columbus.* The two hours were well spent reading and relaxing in the comfortable lobby.

The ADO bus pulled out just before noon. After a few miles we left the city and entered the dual, four-lane, center-divided toll road. The road was a black ribbon that cut across an endless green semitropical landscape. The driver held a steady 55 mph as we passed coconut-oil palm trees, seas of sugar cane, citrus orchards and green fields, with white cattle grazing.

My front passenger window gave me both the highway and the window view. My seatmate introduced himself, then promptly adjusted the seat to recline, closed his eyes and dozed off.

In the distance, I could see there was a population center. The town itself was invisible. Rich, thick green woods, tall brush and vegetation obscured details of the town, but like an atoll in this green sea, a church tower and dome stood out.

The bus bobbed and weaved on the highway. The windshield ploughed the humid air and accumulated a speckled abundance of dead insects.

When we left Córdoba the sky glowed grey, but as the bus traveled south, the glow darkened and then disappeared. Black rain began, first falling lightly and then pelting us with huge drops.

My seatmate woke up. I asked why he was traveling and what his profession was.

"Guillermo Contreras," he introduced himself, "I manufacture perfume and sell."

"How do you make perfume?" I asked.

"Water, alcohol, and concentrated aroma," Guillermo said. "There are about 100 different fragrances." He bought aroma in concentrate, used eight distributors and counted on 500 clients.

From the bus station, in the rain, I caught a taxi to Coatzacoalcos. I wanted to be in the center of town, but in this case I'd be near the port. I asked the cabbie to suggest a hotel. He took me to Valverde. It was reasonable, near the port where a cluster of restaurants offered good meals and an ocean view.

Coatzacoalcos was spread out, a commercial port. Oil and cattle were principal exports. On this rainy day I saw no reason to stay. The most attractive sight was the city bus with a stylized Quetzalcoatl (Feathered Serpent) logo on the side.

Expenses: Meals $21, taxis $4, bus $27, Hotel Valverde $55. Total: $107.

DAY 23
Tuxtla Gutierrez, Marimba Museum

Bus Journey across Mexico

My vintage 2000 map didn't show the new toll highway from Coatzacoalcos to Tuxtla Gutierrez that cut the time and distance in half. I was told that it was a beautiful, scenic route, but "El camino es muy feo," (That's an ugly road). I went to bed puzzled with the words "ugly road" describing a new toll road on my mind.

I caught the bus for Tuxtla Gutierrez in the dark at 5 a.m. and found that "ugly," was the right adjective. The new toll road was already worn out, pockmarked. Heavy oil-service trucks had beaten the highway into a potholed obstacle course.

Juan Carlos, the bus driver, enjoyed the challenge, swerving the bus like a kid playing with a Game Boy and earning points for every missed pothole. Still, time and distance were saved versus the old route. The bus climbed into mountains, and we looked out over lakes and rivers. We crossed Grijalva River. It was cold so I took my sweater from my bag. Profuse vegetation with broad-leafed plants and vines vied with one another for growing space.

The bus descended into the Chiapas Valley. Blue skies, puffy white clouds and warm weather returned.

From the terminal I hailed a cab and said, "I want to go the center." I asked the driver to suggest economical hotel.

"Hotel del Carmen," he said.

It was the best taxi recommendation I'd had in years. Hotel del Carmen greeted me with friendly employees and tasteful décor. It was located two blocks from the park where marimba music played nightly. In the hotel lobby, red poinsettias and a green Christmas tree cheered guests.

Single rooms were listed twice. Like Coca-Cola, Hotel del Carmen offered Single Classic at $28 and Single Premium for $38.

"What's the difference?" I asked.

Mary, the hotel clerk said, "All the rooms are the same. Premium has air-conditioning." I didn't think that heat would be a great inconvenience in December. I took the Single Classic.

None of the rooms had hot water for simply washing, but all showers had hot water. I marveled with curiosity why such an attractive hotel lacked a hot water connection to the bathroom sink.

After a five-hour bus ride, I was ready for a walk so I strolled to the tourist office, which was located in the nearby park. The young lady gave me a map, mentioned the Marimba Museum and circled Instituto de las Artesanias, Centro de Distribucion. Both were within walking distance. In fact, most of the monuments are along Avenida Principal, so a walk broke sightseeing into pleasant stops.

My curiosity was piqued by the Marimba Museum. I always  thought of marimba and Veracruz as synonymous. The museum charged $5, somewhat high for a limited museum in Mexico, but the price included Benjamin Escobedo, an exceptionally well-informed and enthusiastic guide.

The museum tour started with the introduction and evolution of the marimba from Africa. Benjamin explained how African slaves adapted New-World materials that were influenced by Mayans. He detailed the evolution, the history, composers, players and makers of the marimba. Computers offered music and photos of performers. Then Benjamin took me into the workshop where a full-time restorer was working on one of the great classic instruments I had seen in old photos.

I felt like I had an advanced course in marimba history and instrumentology. I offered Benjamin a tip. But he absolutely, palms up, turned me down. "I'm a municipal employee. I earn a salary," he said. I thanked him, yet his knowledge and enthusiasm still made me feel indebted.

I walked down Avenida Principal and passed many attractive restaurants and a few quality hotels. I took photos of an outdoor mural, an artistic mosaic history of Chiapas, on the side of the Universidad de Ciencias y Artes de Chiapas. I climbed to the top of the Morelos Park, with its monument dedicated to the Mexican flag. After catching my breath, I continued down Avenida Principal to the Instituto de las Artesanias. Although only handcrafts

from the State of Chiapas are on display and for sale, the collection is immense and of the highest quality.

Shoppers beware! Traveling by bus forces economical shopping but brings regrets for the items one can't purchase and carry home.

Hotel del Carmen was near the park. Music and dancing in the park were a joy every evening in Tuxtla Gutierrez. The young watched and listened. Older couples put on a graceful and sometimes energetic show. The marimba band started at 6 p.m. A female voice announced the program, then added, "An evening of romantic music, love is in the air, he's on the loose, careful, you may fall in love."

I walked to a nearby restaurant, ordered supper and was drinking a beer when I noticed that the TV in the restaurant was tuned to the local channel, and it was broadcasting live from the park. I mentioned to the waitress that the oldsters danced and the young watched. "Young couples dance after 7 p.m. when the broadcast stops. *Jovenes* (the young) are shy about who they are seen with."

The marimba band played danzón for the first hour, took a break, and then mixed the dance music: salsa, mambo, cha-cha, and

cumbia. I returned to watch and listen. Younger couples were dancing.

Tuxtla is Mayan for rabbit. This once must have been a valley overrun with hares. Gutierrez was both a general and governor of Chiapas. Often Mexican cities honor their history by adding a hero's name to the city.

Expenses: Taxis $2, bus $16, meals $20, Hotel Del Carmen $27, Total: $65.

DAY 24
Tuxtla Gutierrez, City Tour, Zoo, Sumidero Canyon

Bus Journey across Mexico

The next day, Hotel del Carmen was booked for a tour, and I had to move. Santa Maria Hotel, in front of the park, was nearby. Its rate was 50 percent more than Hotel del Carmen and 50 percent less attractive. But it was clean and convenient.

I was told, "You must visit Tuxtla Gutierrez." But my interest was not for the city, but for the zoo and Sumidero Canyon. Both were a surprise to me.

I signed up for an all-day tour. In the morning I had a private guide, Roberto, for the zoological garden. He was pleasant and seemed to assume that I would enjoy the zoo without commentary. His lack of enthusiasm was in contrast with yesterday's Marimba Museum guide. But if I asked, Roberto was helpful. He had a keen eye, spotted animals in the trees and bush and pointed them out to me.

The Miguel Alvarado del Toro Zoo was large, designed to recreate an animal's habitat, and displayed an incredible diversity. Roberto said, "It has the greatest number of species for any zoo in North America." Spiders and snakes were so well represented that I felt creepy about walking in the jungle.

When we finished the zoo tour, Roberto drove me to a number of lookouts over Sumidero Canyon. The vertical drops, sheer walls, and narrow canyon were the result of a rift in the earth's surface. I peered down, over 1000 feet from top of the cliff to the river below. A restaurant with an incredible view was perched on the highest overlook.

From the heights, we retraced part of the road and headed for the depths of the canyon. Robert took me to a river launch boat company and said he'd wait the two hours while I took a fifteen-mile ride between the narrow canyon walls to the hydroelectric dam that filled the canyon and made boating possible.

I joined an international group, two Germans, two Finns, two Spaniards, one Swede, one Mexican and me. The Swedish man and the Mexican woman were newlyweds. Both were close to forty. I asked, "How did you meet?"

The woman said, "Over the Internet. My husband is the second best psychic in Sweden."

Course I wondered who was the best psychic, but I did not ask. They claimed they were soul mates and lovers in a past life and were experiencing the joy and happiness of a second life together. They gave credit to Internet technology, but disagreed about how long they had emailed one another until they met in person.

Our helmsman revved the outboard motor, and we raced between the canyon walls.

He slowed, circled and pointed out crocodiles. Then we neared a rookery of black vultures; hundreds of them had taken up squatters' rights on the white limestone riverbank. They paid us no attention. White on black was an eerie picture.

We cruised toward the hydroelectric dam. We stopped to view natural features, a cave, and an outcropping looking like the face of a crucified Christ. A natural spring trickled down the canyon wall and watered a large moss growth that stood out on the wall looking like a multistory Christmas tree.

Near the dam, two flocks of birds circled and dived for food. There were so many birds that the scene appeared prehistoric. The roar of the outboard motor drove them off. Our guide stopped the launch, explained the history of the dam and mentioned that it is the largest producer of electricity in Mexico.

Sumidero Canyon is a wonder. It's hard to say if it's more spectacular from above looking down, or from below looking towards the sky.

Expenses: Tour $40, meals $23, Hotel Santa Maria $43, Total: $106.

DAY 25
San Cristóbal de Las Casas, Chiapas

Bus Journey across Mexico

The next morning I was up early and on the *colectivo* van (mini bus) headed to San Cristóbal de Las Casas.

San Cristóbal was Mayan country. Indigenous folk, dressed in bright blues, greens, oranges, yellows and reds, were a major percentage of the population. Ancient, artistic hippies from the

1960s, who had once "turned on, tuned in and dropped out," and now had a commercial bent, made San Cristóbal their home and ran bed and breakfast inns. I remembered hippies in San Francisco buying old clothes from Goodwill and second-hand stores, mixing and matching, creating colorful apparel. Now the garments appeared new and the wearer old. Europeans, too, crowded the streets; they came looking for culture. Americans were few; they preferred beaches.

San Cristóbal was a checkerboard of colonial mansions converted into hotels, coffee shops, Internet cafes, indigenous handcraft stores, amber shops, and restaurants. Based on general appearance, hotels offered excellent prices.

From the van drop-off, I walked towards the center of town checking hotels and rates. Hotel La Noria was near to downtown and seemed especially nice and reasonable. I checked in, left my bag and walked to the tourist office.

The tourist office provided me with suggestions and a map. My first visit was to the Museo Ambar (Amber Museum). The museum guide said, "The amber mine is about a four-hour drive from San Cristóbal de Las Casas." The museum was modest in size but had a variety of pieces from the mine. I enjoyed the short presentation, which explained how to tell the difference between real and imitation amber.

The museum guide said that glass and plastic were often sold on the street, and she showed us examples. My eye could not tell real from fake. She held a piece of amber under black light and it phosphoresced. Plastic and glass did not react. "But if you don't have a black light," she said, "you can still judge.

Amber is warm, not cold like glass or plastic. It has an aroma like resin. It burns easily. Tiny insects are embedded, not large ones. A microscope is often needed to view them. And in pure water, amber won't float; add some salt and it may. Rub amber and you'll create static electricity."

I left the Amber Museum and followed the tourist office map past a church and plaza, where handcrafts, blankets, shawls, embroidery in vibrant colores were sold, and headed to the Museo Maya de Medicina. Traditional medicine, both herbs and spells, were important in Chiapas. Herbs cured the body; spells cure the mind; it was psychic medicine.

The Medicina Museum was a large complex. There were attractive dioramas of healers and patients. Plants and herbs were being cultivated in the garden, and each variety was marked with a description: the plant, parts used, and the cure for a particular disease. There was an herb pharmacy and a bookstore.

I looked at my map and chose the next nearest destination, Na-Bolom (House of the Jaguar). Na-Bolom was the private home of Franz Blom, an archeologist, and was filled, room-by-room, with his personal collection. It is now a study and cultural center.

213

There was a notice on a corkboard. The public was invited to dine in the original dining room, but reservations were required. I walked back to the entrance and made a reservation. It was a fixed-price menu and dinner was at 7 p.m.

Dinner was the highlight of the day. I sat at a table for twenty-eight, and I dined alone! When I returned at 7 p.m., two cooks and a waiter were ready for me. I was their only customer. For effect, the waiter set the table for two, with blue and red place settings. I sat at the head of the long empty table. I had a warm fire and a Mayan wall tapestry for company.

Fixed Menu: vegetable soup, tossed iceberg salad (large enough for a family) with a secret sauce, two slices of crumbly bread, frozen butter, mashed potatoes without gravy and sliced beef. I ordered one margarita and got two. There were two pastries for dessert. The bill: $18.

Expenses: Van $4, meals $27, Hotel La Noria $30, Total: $61.

DAY 26
San Cristóbal de Las Casas, San Juan Chamula

Bus Journey across Mexico

This was an intensive trip. I was traveling faster than I could write, with no time to see or digest it all. I was on the run from 6 a.m. to midnight. It was good for my health since I didn't snack and I slept well.

I signed up for a half-day tour, a visit to Chamula, which has become a destination in itself due to its blend of pagan and Catholic rites. Victor, our guide, knew as much as any anthropologist about the people. He had even spent two years providing assistance and liaison to the Spanish newspaper correspondent Valentino Diaz in his contacts with Sub-comandante Marcos, the Chiapas rebel leader.

Chamula is six miles and centuries apart from San Cristóbal. At the edge of town, we stopped at a cemetery silhouetted by a burned out shell of a church that stood silently in back of the graveyard. Many graves were brown, covered with pine needles. Victor said, "Pine needles connect people with the earth. In homes needles are spread on the floor."

Victor explained why the church was a forlorn skeleton. He said, "Too many pine needles, too many candles, and too much liquor." He pointed out the crosses in the cemetery, "White for innocent children, blue or green for adults, black signifies old age, and the ones with rounded tops identify a Mayan."

I mentioned syncretism. Victor took offense and said, "Son Cathólicos! Con sus propios gustos. (They are Catholics! With their own preferences.)"

We drove into Chamula, parked near Templo San Juan and entered the church. It was brilliantly lit with thousands of candles. Photographs were forbidden. There were large pictures of saints around the church, and many groups seated on the floor were clustered here and there, conducting their own services. Shamans and healers had replaced priests.

It was a special province. A resident priest was not allowed. Victor said, "Only visiting priests are allowed to come for baptisms." John the Baptist and saints were venerated here. Believers sat cross-legged on the floor and were staring and self-confessing into mirrors. Shamans conducted rituals with live chickens. Evil spirits were coaxed from the ill, and the suffering transmigrated into a chicken. Later the chicken was strangled. There were traditional herbs, Mayan medicines and psychic cures.

Coca Cola bottles stood out incongruently. Victor said, "Worshipers drink Coke and tequila and bring food. The food and drink nourishes the gods and saints. Mayans believe in reincarnation, and the gods passing through need energy for their long journeys. Coke helps the believer to burp out, to purify himself from evil spirits."

We left the church. Victor said, "Take a walk through the open-air market. It's very colorful. We'll meet at the van in thirty minutes. Then drive to Zincanta for lunch."

The market was a shambles and a rainbow of colors.

Expenses: Tour: Chamula and Zincanta $15, meals $24, Hotel La Noria $30, Total: $69.

DAY 27
Agua Azul, Misol-Ha, Palenque

There was a winding, mountainous, jungle highway, between San Cristobal and Palenque, where nature created two spectacular water cascades, Agua Azul (Blue Water) and Misol-Ha (Water Falls).

These two wonderlands, whitewater churning over boulders, with torrents falling and spray rising, are missed if one takes a bus. You need to stop and make a side trip to enjoy the nature paths that follow the rivers through the shaded forest. Trails lead to calm, still-water pools with sandy beaches. It's a paradise that entices swimmers, mostly stoic Europeans, determined to ignore the chilly water for the memory and a beautiful photo framed by green jungle flora, broad-leafed plants, a mix of tall and spreading trees, with a background of a cascading whitewater curtain.

The clerk at the tourist office in Tuxtla suggested Tratamundo (Globetrotters) Tours and Travel. She said, "They will take you to Agua Azul, Misol-Ha and Palenque, and if you wish they will drop you off in Palenque." That sounded like "two birds, one stone."

223

The cost of a direct bus ticket from Tuxtla to Palenque was $12. The traveler would still have to taxi out to Palenque's Mayan ruins and miss Agua Azul and Misol-Ha. Tratamundo Tours offered all three sites and a drop-off in the town of Palenque for $28. I signed up with Tratamundo. Rafael, the  driver, said, "It will be a long day, 210 kilometers and 210 *topes* (speed bumps that slow traffic passing through villages)."

Palenque, once lost and buried in jungle overgrowth, was excavated in the 1940s. In 1952 Alberto Ruz Lhuillie, an archeologist, was curious about a slab floor inside the Temple of Inscriptions atop the pyramid. He removed the floor and discovered a corbelled arched tunnel. The tunnel led from the top of the pyramid to below a ground-level tomb. Here he found the Tomb of Pakal sealed in a massive, richly carved stone sarcophagus.

A photo of Pakal's sarcophagus lid was used on the cover of Erich von Daniken's book, *Chariots of the Gods*. Von Daniken hypothesized that ancient astronauts helped build the pyramids.

Inspired by von Daniken's description, I took my family to Palenque in June 1975. We boarded a train in Mexico City and jostled to Palenque on a train filled with soldiers. It was a twenty-four-hour ride. We were privileged to ride in old Pullman sleeper cars. The soldiers had to sleep on non-reclining, wooden-slatted seats. Now the roads are better, buses excellent, and there are no more passenger trains.

On the day of our visit in 1975, my family of six accounted for most of the visitors who came to see and explore Palenque. My children, then ages eight and six, and I climbed the pyramid and descended the narrow, slippery, with seeping-water, staircase to Pakal's tomb. Inscribed on the edge of the sarcophagus lid is the genealogy of Pakal, who lived from 603 to 683 AD, ascended the throne in 615 and reigned for sixty-eight years.

Temples and courtyards were adorned with Mayan bas-reliefs, which told of the Mayan view of the cosmos and a history of Palenque. The palace, with a square top, looked like a Spanish church tower without a bell. Today, I was surprised to find Palenque well maintained, with a visitor's center, but some sections were roped off. The pyramid is now off limits to climbers, and the entrance to Pakal's tomb is once again sealed.

At the end of the day, Tratamundo dropped me off in the town of Palenque. I was happy to avoid the three-hour ride back to Tuxtla and the *topes*. It was late, but there was still light. In the main square they were preparing for the celebration of the Virgin of Guadalupe.

Expenses: Taxi $2, tour bus $28, meals $20, Hotel Cathedral $17, entrances fees $4. Total: $71.

DAY 28
Yaxchilán and Bonampak

Bus Journey across Mexico

STP (Servicios Turisticos de Palenque) picked me up at 6 a.m. for a trip back in time, to a lost world. We had a long day ahead. Our destinations: Yaxchilán and Bonampak.

This was European backpack country, few Americans, but today my seatmate was Deborah, a health benefits administrator from Wisconsin, who was traveling alone. We were a mixed group, English, Spanish, Italian, Mexican, and a German, mostly couples. Europeans seek cultural adventures, and Mexico is "land exotic" to them.

I mentioned to the driver, "Looks like a new road."

"It's the Marcos Highway," he said. "The government built this road after Marcos led the Chiapas uprising. And the highway opened up tourism to Bonampak, which was only accessible by light plane before. There are still no paved roads to Yaxchilán. We have to take a river launch, fourteen miles up the Usumacinta River (River of Monkeys)."

We stopped for breakfast. It was now light, the sky a brilliant blue, the jungle a rich emerald green. It was humid but not hot. We got back into our van for a short drive to Mexico's most voluminous

river and looked across the river at Guatemala. Slender launches, more like bullets than boats, maybe four feet wide and twenty feet long with outboard motors, were tied up to an improvised wharf. We were given life vests; we sat on benches facing each other. A palm-arched canopy protected us from the sun.

Our pilot started the engine, and we raced full throttle west, gliding over the smooth flowing river. We passed a Guatemalan military camp. The river snaked, but our pilot straightened his course by cutting across the river's centerline, our straight line crossing an imaginary zigzagged Mexico-Guatemala frontier.

I didn't know what to expect of Yaxchilán. It was new to me. I asked our guide, "What does Yaxchilán mean?"

"Place of the green stones, jadeite," he said. "Precious stones."

The pilot slowed and turned. He pointed out a crocodile and then revved the engine again. He cut the engine, and we could see our landing site. He let the nose of the launch glide into the soft sandy riverbank, and we entered a Lost World. Mayan complexes,

temples, ball courts appeared nearly new, having been renovated by archeologists, but as I walked the trail to the Yaxchilán complex I felt like a member of the scouting party in the original King Kong movie entering a prehistoric world.

Everywhere, I stepped on stones held tight by roots. I looked at the jungle flora, large-leafed plants, vines, everything green and shaded. There was a chattering racket of unseen howler monkeys in the distance, but near the temples and stone monuments with irregular stone steps, five spider monkeys fretted overhead and dropped leaves on our group.

We were explorers. There was not a tourist bus or road in sight. I climbed the highest pyramid. The steps were uneven, irregular and slick. A hill rose beyond the top of the temple. I suspected archeologists have more work ahead. From the top I looked down over the ball court, ruins, and a stele, the tallest in Mexico. Except for the immediate area, all was jungle canopy. I wondered if once the jungle was slashed and burned and planted in corn, beans and squash.

We left this Lost World, retraced the river route, got back in our van and headed for Bonampak, which was now available to the casual traveler. There was airfield, a strip cleared in the jungle, where an abandoned, derelict light plane marked the old landing field. I asked the guide about the plane. "The motor. No good.

And flights aren't profitable since the highway. So when it broke, they left it."

Bonampak's colorful murals attracted visitors. "The best in Mexico," said my guide. "No flash. They will take your camera. No accidents accepted." Two guards watched over us, and we were not permitted to carry our backpacks or shoulder bags inside the small temples. Although there were protective barriers, they did not wish to risk accidental careless scratches from eager visitors. I looked at the murals' bright colors. They told a story. There was a parade of lords and prisoners, bloodletting, torture and sacrifice.

Expenses: Tour, meals included, $60, fees $4, Hotel Cathedral $17. Total: $81.

DAY 29
Campeche: The New Is Old

Bus Journey across Mexico

Days are hot and humid. But the mornings are cool. While getting dressed, I debated whether to wear both a t-shirt and a long-sleeved shirt on the bus. I arrived at the bus station a little late, but just in time to grab one of the last three seats on the 7 a.m. ADO bus for Campeche, a six-hour ride. Great luck, there was a window seat. I snagged it then dozed nearly the whole way, missing the scenery.

Once aboard the bus, the driver revved the engine, turned on the air-conditioning, and I had to get my sweater out of my luggage. And for added irony the movie on the bus was the *March of the Penguins*.

Campeche is not the dreary port town I visited thirty-five years ago when the ocean frontage was merely beachside rubble, and grey was the dominant city color. Mexico has discovered its architectural heritage and the beauty of illumination. Restoration is an industry: archeological, Spanish Colonial, Porfiato haciendas. Campeche, state and city, has invested much capital in restoration projects.

235

Campeche is now graced with an attractive three-mile *malecón*, a wide curving walking, skating, bicycling and jogging path that follows the natural shoreline. Modern sculptures, rest stops and *miramars* are attractively placed along the path. Campeche is a UNESCO World Heritage City. The original fortress colonial city was completely walled, protected by massive stone ramparts, towers and cannons to shield Campeche from pirates.

Much of the original wall, six-sided and in the form of a boat with two bows, still stands guard, cupping Campeche's colonial center. Arched entrances are an attractive feature.

You can walk a section of the ramparts. A gatekeeper charges a fee, locks you in and says, "There is a bell over the entrance; when you're ready to leave, ring the bell." From the ramparts, you view the city, and amazingly you're looking over and behind the city's street walls, and so much terrain is abandoned and neglected. There are acres within the old city that are ready for renewal and development.

When UNESCO added Campeche to its World Heritage list in 1999, the city was reborn in the past. It took two years to remove all telephone poles, overhead lines and cables and bury them underground. Building facades were painted pastel blue, green, rose, yellow and white, and the original decorative elements were emphasized. The library, once the City Hall, was completely restored and the *portales* illuminated. Street lamps, hung from wrought iron supports, were attached to stonewalls. Signs no longer protruded out into the streets. Building facades were easy to see and appreciate.

The cathedral was also cleaned and illuminated and the central park restored. A new kiosk was built in the center of the square. Outdoor tables and restaurant service are offered under its protective roof.

Bordering the central park, Casa Número 6, once a splendid house with arabesque arches, had fallen into decay. Over the years it had served a variety of commercial uses, including a cantina and a furniture store. It is now the Centro Cultural. Pre-restoration photos look more like a Mayan ruin than a city mansion. Today artists perform her and downstairs rooms display period furniture.

What's new in Campeche is, "The Old." Restorations stand out. Fortifications that once protected the city with cannons are now museums with Mayan artifacts.

Thirty years ago, Uxmal, Chichen Itza and Palenque were the featured archeological sites. Now the Yucatan is peppered with "new" sites and Edzna, which I had never heard of, has a sound and light program on Friday nights. Haciendas have been restored and converted into luxury hotels, and colonial churches are being refurbished. The old is rapidly becoming the new.

In 1975 my family and I stayed at El Señorial Hotel, originally the Carvajal family mansion. Now it is government owned. Our spacious bedrooms have been subdivided into offices. But the arabesque arches, curling stairway with wrought iron banisters and patio, are present and cared for.

I recalled a hostile reception in Yucatan thirty-five years ago when a woman gratuitously mocked me on the street as a tourist. She said, "Usted es un tonto (You're stupid)." My reply was, "Porqué? (Why?)," and her swift rebuttal was, "Porqué es (Because you are)." But now, friendliness defined this trip.

In 1975 on the weekend, it was near impossible to exchange $50 in Campeche. Of course there were no ATMs, and there was little acceptance of credit cards. My family had walked the beach, not a paved *malecón* with bike and jogging trails, and decorative monumental art. What hasn't changed? Humidity.

I arrived on December 12, the Day of the Virgin of Guadalupe, and paid my respects. Flowers and candles overwhelmed the Virgin's altar. But my arrival was also in the midst of the book fair and the International Music Festival. There were multiple events to choose from: poets and ballet, romance singers, painters, a pianist, outdoor theater and indoor drama. Spain was the featured honored guest.

I checked in at Hotel Lopez and became the first guest in a newly renovated room with a newly tiled floor, fresh paint, new bath, tile and fixtures. I'd forgotten how nice it is to slip between brand new crisp sheets. All the room lacked was pictures on the wall.

The next day I planned to go to the theater. Because Spain was being honored, Federico García Lorca's play *La Casa de la Senora Alba* was the signature production.

Expenses: Taxi $5, bus $20, meals $19, Hotel Lopez $38. Total: $82.

DAY 30
Campeche International Festival

Bus Journey across Mexico

The dawn-to-dusk excursions, bus rides and tours took some zip out of me. I was glad to spend a few days in Campeche.

Posters advertised the 10th International Festival. Admission to Garcia Lorca's *Casa de la Señora Alba* was free. The drama of a tyrannical mother stifling her five daughters' romantic lives relied too much on shouting sisters to convince me that they were intimidated. I thought, "Couldn't their repression be calm and subtle?"

The housekeeper provided comedy relief. Her best line was, "Two weeks after the wedding, the husband abandons the bed for the dining table."

The commentary about the play said it was an antigovernment metaphor for physical, mental and spiritual repression. But the sisters' romantic frustration seemed less political than a statement of Lorca's personal conflicts, repression and desire. Since the drama was written in early 1936, before Franco ruled Spain, I wondered whether Lorca's metaphor and target was more aptly the Catholic Mother Church.

I took an evening walk. The city glowed, illuminated. There were dancing water fountains in a rainbow of colors. The central plaza was an open stage, crowded with spectators watching a folk ballet. Crafts and art were on display. There was a humorous art show, both educational and cartoonish.

The best exhibit was a collection of satiric caricatures of pirates, not Blackbeard or Captain Blood of the past, but commercial CD music and intellectual property pirates. I wanted to take photos of the best jabs at the pirate vendors, but then I would be a pirate. They were good, so clever, ethically instructive, and satirically funny without falling into nasty finger pointing.

Concerts were free. Raúl Simón, the Argentine romantic ballad singer, performed in one of the rooms at the Casa Cultural where a book fair was also in progress. I had never heard of Raúl Simón, but when he sang he encouraged his audience to sing along, and to my surprise, he had a very supporting chorus. His songs were popular.

I visited the Immaculate Conception cathedral. Its treasure is a silver ark showing in detail, step-by-step, the crucifixion of Christ. I walked around the ark as if it were the Stations of the Cross. Here was the story of Christ's last suffering from the 30 pieces of silver to the cock that crowed three times.

Expenses: Walking free, meals $17, Hotel Lopez $38. Total: $55.

DAY 31
Campeche, Edzna and Slapstick Comedy

Bus Journey across Mexico

It could have been a set-up by the Keystone Cops. Today started with slapstick comedy, a whirl of confusion and everyone wanted to help, but they all pointed in different directions!

Last night I asked about a tour to Edzna, a Mayan city spread over five square miles, with a huge ball court, a monument decorated with two colorful carved masks and a stone staircase leading to a high temple overlooking a sea-green canopy of jungle trees. Mary, the receptionist at Hotel Lopez, phoned Xtampak Tours. "It's a

four-hour tour. They leave at 9 a.m., the price is 150 pesos ($15), but the minimum is two tourists. Would you pay 300?" I said, "Maybe by 9 a.m. tomorrow they will have another passenger." I let it go.

I wanted to leave earlier, and the Central Terminal had a bus leaving at 8 a.m. for 120 pesos, round trip. Of course, I'd have to get myself to the terminal.

Up at 6:30 a.m., coffee for breakfast and with a map in hand, I walked, headed for the Central Terminal. I came to a *glorieta* (traffic circle) with its multiple spokes. As I perused my map, a young man asked me where I wanted to go. "Camionero Central," I said.

He waved his hand, pointing beyond the *glorieta* and said, "Detras, detras (behind, behind)."

I crossed the street and there was no access to "behind." I had walked a block east, now I had to retrace my steps and go two blocks west where I found "behind," a city bus stop that would take me to the Central Terminal.

245

I arrived twenty minutes before the 8 a.m. departure. I went over to ADO First Class window and asked for a round trip ticket for Edzna. "Sorry, that bus has been canceled today. You'll have to go to South Terminal, Second Class."

Showing my map, I asked directions. The clerk looked at the map, saw a bus icon, and pointed, "Here." It wasn't too far.

I caught a second city bus and told the driver I wanted to go to "South Terminal."

He said I'd have to transfer. "Here" was not South Terminal!

I mentioned that I was trying to go to Edzna. A man, with some English, volunteered, "You want to get off at the *Mercado* and take a *colectivo* (minivan)." The *Mercado* was also the transfer point. I got off the bus and started to look for a *colectivo*.

A woman, who was on her way to work, overheard. She said, "Let me take you, it's on my way."

I said, "I want to go to Edzna."

She insisted that South Terminal was where I should buy a ticket. I didn't want to appear rude, so I followed her, and we got on the next bus to South Terminal.

She told me to go to the ADO Second Class window and left for her office. At the ADO window I asked for a ticket to Edzna and was told, "No, you have to take a *colectivo*."

Another woman stepped forward and spoke in English. "You need ticket bus." That phrase sounded strange to me. She said, "Take a taxi to ticket bus." I wrote it down on the same paper that said Central Terminal.

I asked her, "Is ticket bus the right word in Spanish?"

"Yes, yes, ticket bus."

In front of the bus terminal a taxi driver was anxious for a fare. I asked if he could take me to "ticket bus." That confused him. My request and accent made no sense to him. I tried to explain about Edzna, the *colectivo*.

He saw my note, took it out of my hand and spoke with another driver. "Yes, I can take you." I got in the taxi, and he started to drive to Central Terminal.

I jabbered, not very coherently, about the *Mercado* where I had transferred and maybe there would be colectivos. Finally, I pointed the way and took my chances.

At the Mercado, I left the taxi, and a few questions later I found the *colectivos*. But the Edzna colectivo would not leave until 10 a.m. It was only 8:25 a.m. All the buses, taxis, help and mistakes were so efficient that I hadn't lost much time. I was ten blocks from Hotel Lopez, plenty of time to walk back and hope for a tour to Edzna.

At five to nine, I asked Mary if I could still catch a tour to Edzna. She phoned Xtampak Tours. "You're the only one, would you pay 250 pesos?" she asked.

"Fine," I said.

"The guide will pick you up in fifteen to twenty minutes," she said.

The hotel restaurant was now open and I'd have just enough time for a quick breakfast in the hotel's cafe. I ordered and said, "Rush, please."

The coffee came instantly, but it was too hot to drink. I could hear the cook scrambling my eggs when Mary came into the cafe and said, "The driver has arrived." It hadn't been five minutes since Mary hung up the phone.

"Can he wait?" I asked.

Mary said, "He can't park. He'll have to go around the block."

I rushed back to the waitress and asked for my breakfast to go. The tour guide made a quick circle around the block. I entered his car holding a Styrofoam box with eggs, beans and toast, but no coffee. It was still scalding. I thought of the McDonald's incident, and I didn't want to spill the hot coffee, so I left it.

It was a forty-minute drive on a good two-lane road, with hardly any traffic to Edzna. My guide was really only a driver. He would wait for two hours while I visited the site. I paid the 33 pesos entry and found myself nearly alone in Edzna.

There were only three other visitors and a gardener riding a lawnmower, trimming the football-sized grass field in front of the main temple. I did not tarry. I read each description, climbed the temple's steep staircase and photographed the chromatic masks carved in the monument.

Included in the description of the Maya's culture and achievements, was the disclaimer, "The Maya were never helped by extraterrestrial beings." Someone was concerned that Erich von Daniken's bestselling book, "*Chariots of the Gods*" and his hypothesis that astronauts built the pyramids, would discredit Mayan achievement. I finished my self-guided tour in an hour, and my driver Juan was pleased to return early to Campeche.

Expenses: Taxi $3, City buses $1, Meals $29, Tour Edzna $30, Hotel Lopez $38, Total: $101

DAY 32
Hacienda Uayamon Wedding Day
This is so romantic!

Bus Journey across Mexico

While checking the Ourmexico.com Forum website in October, I was intrigued by a request. An English couple was planning their wedding, getting married at a hacienda in Campeche. They requested a photographer, but not a professional package deal. They asked if someone casual, a traveler, might be in the area December 15th and would like to photograph their nuptials.

I emailed Sabrina and Jaime, mentioning that I had experience taking wedding photos since the '60s when outdoor hippy weddings were in vogue, at least among my friends. I said, "I'm an amateur with experience, and my price is free." We exchanged emails. I told them that Campeche was on my Bus Journey Across Mexico itinerary, and that I had a special interest in restored haciendas. They accepted my offer, and I advanced my planned trip from January to December.

I'd arrived in Campeche December 13, two days before the wedding. Sabrina and Jaime were already in Campeche, staying at the Sir Francis Drake Hotel. I'd tried to get a room at Sir Francis, but they were booked for the weekend and I could only stay three nights. I asked, "Could you suggest another hotel?"

The bellman immediately volunteered, "Hotel Lopez, one block." He pointed to the right. "It's very good and economical," he said.

Hotel Lopez was a perfect recommendation. I saved 30%, and I was the first guest in a completely remodeled room. The bath was newly retiled, and in Mexico that means floor, walls and ceiling. The fixtures were new. The bedroom smelled lightly of fresh paint, and the bedroom floor was also newly tiled. The room lacked pictures and wall decorations, but I was thrilled when I climbed into bed that night between new sheets.

I contacted Sabrina and Jaime, and the next morning we met for breakfast. After the wedding, they were moving to Italy. They explained that the wedding would be at 5 p.m. Jaime had an unusual camera, a Lomo, which had a special lens. Colors would be saturated in the center and the edges of the photos tended to fade to dark. Jaime said, "The Lomo prints appear magical, like a dream."

I would be taking pictures without a flash, using a manual focus setting, click and wind camera. I'm a point and shoot photographer, and I was concerned that I might spoil the photos because of being inexperienced with the camera. I said, "I'll use two cameras." My digital Fuji is low light with an auto focus.

We discussed the travails of getting married in Mexico. "A blood test is a must," said Sabrina. "And there always seems to be another piece of necessary paperwork." They also hired a translator. I said, "The ceremony will be repeated." I felt good about that. I'd have a chance to snap each picture twice.

Saturday we met at the Sir Francis Drake Hotel at 2 p.m. Sabrina would have her hair done at the hacienda. She wanted a '50s look, and her hair stylist had volunteered to drive us. We arrived at Uayamon Hacienda, a Starwood boutique resort. There were only twelve rooms; most were cottages, very private, on the grounds of a partially restored hacienda.

The weather had taken a turn. There was light drizzle. Umbrellas greeted us. Wolfgang Kresse, hotel manager, introduced the staff and offered us champagne. Sabrina and Jaime checked in and were escorted to separate cottages.

The cottages were once hacienda workers' homes, but now they were luxury units, with spacious baths and dual vanities. Roses were set out everywhere. They decorated the bath, added a touch of red to the tissue box, gave a soft presence to the wash cloths, accented the silver tray on the coffee table and were sprinkled across the white bed spread.

The rain stopped and I walked the grounds. An abandoned stone storage building, now roofless, had been converted into to a swimming pool with stone columns. Paths led through peaceful gardens. This was a secluded place for private, quiet relaxation.

I met the gardener, Rosendo. He showed me the abandoned chapel and took me to the old hospital, now converted into hotel suites, where the wedding would be held under the archway. I asked Rosendo how long he had worked at Hacienda Uayamon.

"I was born here," he said. "I've worked the hacienda all my life. Now it's a hotel. I planted the *ceiba* tree in the courtyard when I was only twelve. That was sixty-six years ago."

"May I see the tree?" I asked.

"You've seen it!" Rosendo said.

I knew the *ceiba* tree was important to the Mayans, but my book learning lacked practical experience. The *ceiba* is often called "the silk-cotton tree" and its fiber, kapok, is used in sleeping bags. Rosendo took me back to the entrance. The *ceiba* tree, with its huge trunk, towered over the hacienda. From its size I would have guessed it to be three times its age. Rosendo stood dwarfed in front of the massive tree, and I took his picture.

Mayans used five cardinal points, north, south, east, west and center. The ceiba tree represented the center, and its trunk was mystically connected to the different planes of existence.

The wedding was classic, elegantly simple. There were no guests, only a few members of the hotel staff, the hair stylist and her husband, the judge, the translator and me. With daylight ebbing, the ceremony began. As the light faded, the yellow-red flames of torches, symbols of love and desire, slowly broke the darkness, like a blessing and a new beginning. The judge spoke. The words were translated. Sabrina and Jaime repeated the vows. Rings were exchanged. There was joy and smiles and love and happiness.

And then they kissed.

Expenses: Meals $34, Hotel Lopez $38, Total: $72.

DAY 33
Camino Real (Royal Highway), Uxmal Mayan Center, Franciscan Missions, Ruta de Conventos (Route of Convents)

Bus Journey across Mexico

When I mentioned to my friend Bernardo that I was going to Campeche, he said, "I have friends in Campeche. I'll send an email; maybe they can be your guide."

So when I reached Campeche, Alberto and Lirio offered to be my guides and to drive me to Merida. I told Alberto, "I'm interested in haciendas, Mayan ruins and Franciscan missions, especially the largest, the convent at Mani where Bishop Landa burned the Mayan codices."

Albert said, "We can make a tour, part Camino Real, stop at Hacienda Blanca Flor, breakfast in Hecelchakán, then cut over to Uxmal, the Mayan ceremonial center and then continue to Mani, which is on the Ruta de Conventos."

It was an excellent plan. It took us through traditional Mayan areas with thatched huts and into the towns of Santa Elena and Ticul, with their plain fortress churches with few windows, built to withstand Mayan attacks.

We first stopped at Hacienda Blanca Flor, built in the 17th century and used as a stronghold during the War of the Castes in 1843. It was well maintained, owned by a doctor in Campeche and open for tourism and business meetings. Across the road, a haunting church skeleton overshadowed Blanca Flor. Black crows, looking like animated gargoyles, strutted on the roofless walls. I took pictures of the abandoned church, the only part of the hacienda now neglected, the church's rookery an Edgar Allen Poe scene.

Octavio, the manager, guided us around the property. He pointed out the Mayan glyph chiseled in stone above the archway that led to the fields. The glyph was the iconic Mayan harvest god of plenty. Next to the entrance were two statutes, St. Francis and Chac-Mool, the Mayan god of rain. Fresh produce was growing in the hacienda garden. Workers were pulling radishes and cleaning lettuce.

Saddles were lined up in the corridor ready for a mount. An ancient Ford flivver set on blocks added to the sense of antiquity. Tourists were encouraged to stay in the hacienda and take side trips to Mayan ruins, Campeche the Fortress Walled City, Isla Arena (Sand Island) and Gurtas de Loltun (Loltun Grotto).

We got back into Alberto's truck. "Time for breakfast," he said. We left Campeche before 7 a.m., and we were hungry. This was part of Alberto's plan. He had a special place in mind, the outdoor restaurant on the plaza in Hecelchakán. Alberto recommended "*torta cochinita* (thin-sliced pork sandwich)."

In Hecelchakán, the sidewalk was jammed with diners. "This is a popular place," I said.

Alberto said, "People drive all the way from Campeche just for a *torta cochinita.*" We ordered *cochinita*; the marinated sliced pork was folded into a tortilla. I generally have coffee for breakfast, but this savory sandwich called for a beer.

In front of the restaurant, parked side-by-side at the curb, were three-wheel bicycle-taxis. A standard bike frame and back wheel were attached to a two-wheel front cart with a shade roof. Two people could sit together. Shoppers could carry their purchases home.

A bicycle-taxi pulled out, carrying a passenger who was sitting erect with grocery bags at her feet. She held a tray of thirty eggs and appeared unconcerned about her fragile cargo. On the streets these taxis were busy. I wanted a ride.

While we waited for our *tortas*, I asked, "How much for a quick ride to the church and back?" The driver said, "10 pesos ($1)." I hopped in, and Alberto took my picture, enjoying the brief pedal powered ride.

We left the Camino Real and drove to Uxmal.

I had visited Uxmal in 1975 with my family. Uxmal was nearly deserted then, and archeologists were working on the site. Today Uxmal is on the tourist circuit. There are good roads, excellent services, a nearby hotel and restaurants. Much has been restored since 1975, but visitors are no longer allowed to climb the steep steps to the top of the Pyramid of the Magician. "Too many accidents," I was told.

The Pyramid of the Magician (legend says it was conjured up in three days) is my favorite Mayan monument. It leaves me with a sense of awe. It is sheer stone with curved-sides. Its bulk rises dramatically from the flat plain and towers over the jungle canopy as a testament to a once powerful Mayan city-state.

We drove to Mani and passed through Ticul. Life-sized Mayan heroes and gods, statutes looking like kings, stood guard on nearly every corner. A plain church stood in the plaza. The upper façade looked like a brooding, stylized Mayan face glaring from the Catholic fortress. It was afternoon when we arrived in Mani, and the convent was closed until 4 p.m. This once principal town and seat of power was quiet and nearly deserted.

Under the arches of Mani's City Hall there were two eye-catching displays. The brightest, with red flames, was a mural showing Bishop Landa putting the torch to the Mayan idols and codices in 1562. The bishop, interested in saving souls, believed he was destroying the works of the devil.

Mayans seemingly had converted to Christ and Catholicism, but syncretism was the reality. Mayans accepted Christian saints and the Catholic mass as extensions of pre-Hispanic rites and beliefs. But Mayan statues were found secreted in altars and even in the

cross itself. Concerned for Mayan souls, Bishop Landa set an immense bonfire. He incinerated 5000 idols, 197 ceremonial vases and twenty-seven deerskin codex scrolls in an effort to halt Mayan heresy. Mayan history was lost in the conflagration, and today's historians deeply regret this act.

The second eye-catcher, next to the mural of Landa's bonfire, was a group of five recent photos. They pictured step-by-step the annual Mayan ritual ceremony, asking Chac-Mool to bring rain for an abundant harvest. Ironically, after four centuries, Catholic worshipers pray to Chac-Mool. Bishop Landa destroyed the physical but never fully converted the Mayan heart.

In Mani, we lunched at Tutul-Xiu, a giant thatched roofed restaurant with open sides. Shade and breeze are important in this hot, humid climate. I let Alberto order for me. "The specialty of the house," he said. I was served an attractive plate of small, thinly sliced pieces of pork with tomatoes and onions. I ordered Montejo beer, named for the conquistador of Yucatan.

The huge stonewalled Franciscan mission dominated Mani. It was once a fortress, a church, a self-sufficient community, and a seat of government. It has suffered numerous violations, often stripped, and the interior was quite plain. It has been partially restored and there were attractive *retablos* in the church. The open chapel, walled up for centuries, has been reopened. In the garden, an ancient water mill was present, but a modern pump was used to draw the water.

It was after 4 p.m., and it would be dark in an hour. Alberto drove me to Merida, dropped me off on Calle 60, just off the central plaza, where I had my pick of a dozen hotels. I chose the modest Hotel San Juan, $35 a night with pool and air-conditioning. But for $80 I could have stayed at Hotel Mission Merida in real luxury, with a superb pool.

Expenses: (Alberto and Lirio were my guests for meals, and as I was theirs for the day, I had no transportation costs.) Meals $56, fees $26, Hotel San Juan $35, Total: $117.

DAY 34
Merida: Sunday: A Day of Rest

Bus Journey across Mexico

No taxis, no buses, no traveling. It was Sunday. I decided to take a day of rest, a calm walk, a just-to-gawk day, see the people, the kids, the street entertainers, and check my email.

Every Sunday, downtown Merida becomes a pedestrian mall. Barricades are set up, tables set out, stages erected and families come for music, street performers, outdoor dining, and to see clowns entertaining children on the circular stage in the park.

It was a day for an outdoor table, *guacamole*, *totopos* (chips), a cold Montejo beer and people watching. The weather was warm, and the morning fog morphed into a bright blue sky by 10 a.m. Later in the day, I'd have my choice of a children's choir singing Christmas carols in the plaza near my hotel, a symphony in the Teatro Merida, or a contemporary art show.

I preferred to walk rather than sit, so I chose the art show. On my way, I heard part of the children's choir singing, young voices, sweet sopranos and high tenors. Then as I passed the theater, I poked my nose into the lobby. The theater was built in 1949, but it has the grace and style of a movie palace designed in the 1930s. It must be one of the last Art Deco-styled buildings ever built.

The Museo Contemporaneo housed the art show. The museum itself has a colonial-styled arched interior and a central patio with rooms on four sides. A security guard stood at the door in front of each room. As I approached, the guard opened the door. It was warm on the patio, but the room was air-conditioned. The guard was stationed not only to protect the exhibitions but also to see that the air conditioning was not wasted.

In the second room, the featured exhibit started on the left with a photo of a rust-red bison, a drawing from the cave wall at Alta

Mira, Spain. A second photo was of a similar cave drawing from central Baja California discovered in the 1950s. The show was a timeline of art, a record of man's creative expression.

Photographs marched along the walls and up to a second floor and downstairs again. The centerpiece was Michelangelo's masterpiece, titled in Spanish, *"God Giving the Spark of Life to Adam."* Photographs of the world's great art masterpieces were featured in chronological sequence, from the cave drawings, to Greek statues, to Roman mosaics reclaimed from Pompeii, to flat Byzantine iconography, to three-dimensional perspective European Renaissance classics, Dutch and Spanish.

As I looked and walked, I retraced history, yet moved ahead era by era. Modern art added Picasso, Dalí, Miró and the last featured piece was by Frida Kalo. Thus, the exhibit started with a Mexican cave painting and ended with a Mexican artist. I felt like a student who had just prepared for the final exam in Art History 1A.

It was time for another Montejo beer in the park. With my glass of a cold beer, I sat in the park and thought of The *True History of the Conquest of Mexico*, the eyewitness account by Bernal Diaz del Castillo. The Yucatan played a major role. Two Spaniards, Jeronimo Agustin and Gonzalo Guerrero, survivors of a shipwreck and somehow not sacrificed on a Mayan altar, spent five years living with the Mayan. Both learned Mayan and when Cortes sailed the coast, he found them. Jeronimo chose to come with Cortes and ultimately was a key translator during the conquest. Gonzalo elected to stay with his Mayan wife and children. He's considered the Father of the Mestizo Race. I consider him a father who loved his family.

Expenses: Meals $22, Hotel San Juan $35, Total: $57

DAY 35
Chichen Itza-Valladolid-Chetumal

Buses run day and night. I was up at 5 a.m., and it was hard to find a taxi in Merida in the predawn dark. I walked the ten blocks to the bus station and caught the ADO bus for Chichen Itza that left at 6:30 a.m.

After two hours on the bus I later I arrived in Chichen Itza. It was good timing as I arrived ahead of the vanguard of tourist buses and European tour groups. Shops and restaurants weren't open, but the gate to the archeological site was. Tickets cost 95 pesos. "Where can I leave my bag?" I asked. The ticket clerk had to track down security. I was the first to store a bag. In fact, I emptied my shoulder bag into another plastic bag to reduce weight and bulk as I visited Chichen Itza.

I had been here with my family in 1975. Cancun was under construction; tourism was a hope. We had the site mostly to ourselves back then. I don't even recall souvenir vendors.

In 1975 we scaled El Castillo the famous four-sided, ninety-one-step pyramid. (91 x 4= 364, and the platform made it 365.) We climbed every monument and went inside the observatory. Today, hundreds of tour buses, thousands of tourists, visit daily. The parking lot is large enough for tailgating at the Super Bowl. Major monuments are roped off. El Castillo is off limits. With so many visitors, wear and tear and accidents had to be prevented.

Mayan merchants were arriving with their merchandise stacked high on their backs, looking like old photos from a B. Traven novel of overburdened human cargo carriers. Their loads extended above their heads, and the carriers used headbands for support and balance. Vendors picked their place in the shade along the trails of Chichen Itza. Blankets and tarps were laid out to define the boundaries of their store. Hammocks, masks, carved wood and mosaic-stone jewelry, silver and beads of jade and amber were for sale.

Pottery, plates and sarapes, all in brilliant colors, were displayed. There was even a large carved Mayan jaguar for sale. I admired a mask and was impressed by the quality. In fact, most of the handcrafts were attractive, well made and crafted by artisans.

I asked a vendor, "Do you have to have a license to sell inside the park?"

He said, "No, it's a tradition and we have a right. But we are protesting."

"Protesting?" I asked.

"We object to the construction of the *palapas* (large thatched-roofed buildings). They are stealing our business."

"How many merchants are there?" I asked.

"We are 500."

Amazing, I thought, 500 small businesses lining the footpaths of Chichen Itza and threatened by store sales. It's the fear of the small town merchant when WalMart breaks ground.

Having arrived early I was able to see Chichen Itza with few tourists. Because climbing the monuments was now forbidden, the visit went quickly. I read the posted explanations, took photos, and completed the circuit in two hours, just in time to catch the bus for Valladolid.

When I went for a bus ticket, the clerk said, "The bus is just leaving, pay the driver." I raced, running with three bundles, the small suitcase, the plastic bag and my shoulder bag. The bus had just left the yellow zone. I shouted. The Oriente Bus security man put his fingers in his mouth and whistled. His shrill whistle caught the driver's attention. I ran, with my three bags swinging. I must have looked like a panicky St. Nick running after his sleigh. The bus stopped at the gate. I arrived, huffing and puffing. The door opened and I got on. It was air-conditioned. "20 pesos," the driver said.

In less than an hour we arrived in Valladolid. The bus station was only three blocks from this colonial town's main square. I checked the bus schedule. Three hours was enough time to have lunch, visit the city, see San Bernadino de Sisal Convent and the Zaci grotto and *cenote*.

The main plaza looked attractive. Lunch was eaten under the arches next to the City Hall. I ordered a cold beer and *comida* (the meal of the day), breaded beef, rice, beans, tomato and lettuce.

In the City Hall, I found murals depicting the Mayan conquest, enslavement and ultimate liberation. They were educational, vividly colorful and dramatic, but not fine art.

I hailed a taxi. We agreed on $10 for one hour, just enough time to visit the convent, the grotto and *cenote* and then to drop me at the Oriente Bus Depot. Both sites were within walking distance, but in opposite directions. I didn't want to retrace my footsteps, and besides, I was tired of feeling like a pack mule.

272

The cabbie drove down Calzada de Los Frailes to the giant, high-walled San Bernardino de Sisal convent. Like Mani, it was imposing, built to be a church and a convent and to be self-sufficient. It appeared unchanged since its founding in 1552. My first thought was, "This was a fortress." Its façade was a checkerboard pattern devoid of any religious symbols or art. The church was closed. In the rear, there is an ancient, once mule-powered, water wheel where if you looked down, you could see an underground stream.

San Bernardino is one of the examples where Spanish exploitation and Franciscan ministry collided. Franciscans purposely founded their convent away from the Spanish settlers. (This was also true in San Francisco, California, where the mission and the Presidio were built miles apart.) Spanish hacenderos needed labor and resented the Franciscans.

The taxi crossed town and took me to the Zaci grotto and *cenote*. I entered a cavern, followed a trail a short distance and found the

still-water *cenote*. *Cenotes* are natural wells, sink holes that have caved in and exposed underground rivers, a main source of water for the Mayans.

This *cenote* was a natural beauty, not exposed as a deep, giant vertical well like the *cenote* at Chichen Itza, but part of a cavern complex, with an overhanging ledge and a worn trail down to the water's edge.

I passed a number of signs saying, "No Swimming." But, at the foot of the *cenote*, I found five happy bathers. "This water is cool," one bather said. It looked like the perfect refresher for a hot day.

I took pictures and then walked back to my waiting cab. In no time I was back on the bus. It was 2:30 p.m., and I'd reach Chetumal before 8 p.m.

Expenses: Bus $8 to Chichen Itza, $2 to Valladolid, $14 to Chetumal, taxis $12, meals $10, Hotel Arges $39, entrance fees $11. Total: $96.

DAY 36
Chetumal

Bus Journey across Mexico

The Valladolid bus pulled into Chetumal.

I roused myself, left the bus and stood in the taxi line, which moved quickly. I told the driver, "Take me to the center of town," thinking there would be a traditional center. The driver pulled up in front of the Holiday Inn on Avenida Heroes across from the Museo Maya and the tourist office. The Center for the Arts was around the corner.

The "center" of Chetumal was the Mercado, a vast commercial shopping mall. It was active but without charm, and Holiday Inn was not exactly my idea of Mexico. I checked in at the reception desk. I asked the clerk, "Could you suggest an economical hotel?"

Immediately, he recommended a nearby hotel. "Hotel Arges is three blocks toward the bay, on a side street. It's newly remodeled."

Hotel Arges was one-third the price of the Holiday Inn, modest, clean, comfortable and quiet, until my neighbor in the next room turned on the TV at 5 a.m. Noise is tolerated and ignored in Mexico. How it's transmitted and amplified by cement walls is a Mexican mystery.

So, I got an early start. Shops were already opening. Sidewalk vendors were unpacking boxes and setting up displays. There was little traffic on the street. I walked down Avenida Heroes, which took me directly to the bay port and the Centenario Plaza where an obelisk honored the fallen heroes of the 1919-1920 Revolution. Off to the side, band members were gathering under a thatched-roofed bandstand for a practice session.

I arrived at Chetumal Bay and looked across the bay, gazing towards the Caribbean. Belize could be seen in the distance. I had bused across Mexico's extremes, from Tijuana to Chetumal, from north to south, west to east, from the Pacific to the Atlantic. I'd made it from California to Guatemala, and soon I'd claim from Tijuana to Cancun as I traveled north along the Mayan coast and visited Bacalar, Tulum, Playa del Carmen. Then I would fly home from Cancun. I'd explored a vast Mexican mosaic, and I felt a real joy in having accomplished the journey by bus.

I looked over the calm sea, shimmering in the morning light, and I put on my sunglasses. The horizon was a bright blue. It was hot and humid; my cap was damp with sweat.
I reflected that this was once pirate country. I walked the palm- and magnolia-tree-lined bayside paseo. A young couple sat under the shade of a palm tree, he leaning against the sea wall, she against him. A yellow rowboat was beached, turned upside down as if pirates had just landed.

The Palacio Presidential faced the bay. Each story of this three-floor building had a bay-view veranda, and the design reminded me of Queen Kamehameha's Iolani Palace in Honolulu. A sign on the paseo read: Parque Renacimiento (Renaissance Park). I walked a few blocks and found a new Sam's Club and El Poton Restaurant, also owned by WalMart.

I breakfasted at El Fenico (The Phoenician), with ancient sailboats painted on the walls. The restaurant's windows were open to the gentle breeze.

It was now almost 10 a.m. and the Mayan Museum was opened. I was greeted with air-conditioning, nearly too cold. There was a Mayan thatched-hut exhibit in the patio, completely furnished. I joked, "How much to stay the night?"

The Mayan Museum was a combination of Mayan artifacts, models of two important sites, Palenque and Tikal, mural reproductions in vivid colors from Bonampak, Yaxchilán and Caxcala and excellent descriptions of Mayan society, their calendar, numerical system and rituals. The model of Palenque was in the basement but could be viewed through the glass first floor. I didn't walk on the glass, didn't want to smudge the view for others.   It was a unique, effective display.

It was the perfect educational review after having visited Yaxchilán, Edzna, Palenque, Uxmal and Chichen Itza. The museum was a survey and review of all I had seen.

Expenses: Taxi $2, meals $14, Hotel Los Arges $39, museum fee $5, Total: $60.

DAY 37
Bacalar, Tulum, Playa del Carmen

Bus Journey across Mexico

I was nearing the end of my trip. I woke up early, eager to move on. In dawn's light, the sky glowed; the sun was hidden in the fog. I walked six blocks to the *colectivo* (minivan) pick up. There were no vans. It was 6:45 a.m.

I asked a taxi driver if I was in the right place to catch the *colectivo* for Bacalar. "I'll take you for 80 pesos ($8)," he said. Bacalar is a multicolored lagoon known for its star-shaped fort, built to protect the town from pirates. It is also famous for its Agua Azul Cenote (Blue Water Well). It's a forty-minute ride from Chetumal, and I thought $8 was a good price. The *colectivo* would have cost $2.

It was early, no traffic, and we arrived at Agua Azul in less than half an hour. It was still dark as fog shrouded Agua Azul and the sun glowed, appearing to be a full moon reflected on the lake, as if the scene was the sequel to Ansel Adams' prize photo *Moonrise Over Hernandez*. The name of the lake was also the name of the restaurant, which was eclectically decorated with old rifles from the Revolution, live squawking parrots, a mounted bull's head with a hat on each horn, a Mexican sombrero balanced by a

Texas cowboy's hat. It was an open-air restaurant, posts supported the palm-thatched roof, and fans stirred the humid air.

I was their first breakfast diner. Carlos asked if I'd like coffee while I waited for the cook to set up. I said yes, and he brought me a cup of hot water and a jar of Nescafé instant.

The water in the *cenote* was crystal clear, ninety feet deep and actually fed by nine natural springs. A family was already enjoying a swim.

When breakfast arrived, I asked Carlos to call a taxi for me. It was  about a mile to town, and I thought by the time I finished my breakfast the cab would be ready. Perfect timing. The cabbie arrived and we drove into Bacalar. The town was still quiet. The museum would not open for another twenty minutes. I walked around the outside of the old fort. I looked out over the multicolored lagoon. Small boats were for rent, and attractive restaurants and bars were at the water's edge. This was a touch of paradise.

I took a few pictures and went back to the fort-museum. Its theme was pirates, ships and navigation. There were comments about pre-Hispanic Mayan shipping and trade. The displays were written in Spanish and English. It was a relatively small fort and museum, but I marveled that any band of pirates would attack.

I checked the bus schedule. I looked at my watch and scurried to the ADO-Mayab Terminal. I wanted to see Tulum, the Mayan coastal temple and walled citadel. Tulum may have been the

Spaniards' first view of an advanced civilization in the New World. Spaniards were astonished by the stone citadel and compared it to well-built structures in Spain.

From Bacalar, I was in for a three-hour ride. I bought a ticket, but seats were first come first served, and a number of teenagers, on their way to Playa del Carmen for the holidays, had appropriated extra seats. I sat in last row. It was a good choice. The last row sat higher than the rest, and I had a decent view of the highway ahead and a side window too.

I practiced my Spanish with three youngsters aged fifteen, twelve and eleven. They were bright and eager to speak with an old gringo from California.

The bus pulled into Tulum. I expected to be dropped off at the archeological site, not realizing that Tulum was also the name of the local town. I had to catch a taxi for the three-mile ride to the ruins. The driver explained, however, that from Tulum's ruins, I could catch a bus to Playa del Carmen or Cancun. And he said, "Take a *colectivo*; they are more frequent and less expensive."

The taxi dropped me off at the Tulum ruins, but from the entrance, it was still a hike. You can walk or take the train, which is a tractor pulled double-car that transports 100 visitors at a time.

Of all the Mayan temple sites I visited, Palenque, Uxmal, Edzna, Bonampak and Yaxchilán, Tulum was by far the most overrun by tourists. Groups crowded the site. There were more tourists in Tulum than stones in the major temple. The site is virtually roped off to visitors. "See but don't climb," is now the rule. This is also true of Palenque, Uxmal and Chichen Itza. Pogo said it best, ages ago, "We have met the enemy and he is us."

Swimmers climbed down a wooden staircase to the gulf. Soft breakers stirred the shoreline. The ocean offered refreshing relief from the heat and humidity. I read the bilingual commentaries and was thankful I wasn't herded with a group. Europeans outnumbered Americans. The afternoon sun was perfect for photos, but most pictures are sprinkled with tourists.

Tulum is not a large site. One hour is sufficient to walk, read the legends, photograph and even touch your toe into the sand of the Caribbean Sea.

I caught the tractor-train back to the center. Papantla men, *Volantes* (Flyers) performed the high-climbing, swinging-rope ritual. One man stands atop a ninety-foot pole, four others, representing the four cardinal points, perform a ritual, then drop backwards, upside-down, feet attached to ropes and they unwind, circling the ground. The ritual is in reverence to the rain god, and the performers are a metaphor for the falling rain.

I'm afraid of heights, but *Volantes* scurry up a ninety-foot pole and carry out an ancient ritual. I had seen *Volantes* perform at the Aguascaliente Fair, but I did not know their history until now. *Volantes* are Tononac natives that perform a pre-Hispanic fertility rite just outside the main gate.

At the entrance, there is a low modern building, a semicircle of tourist shops that helps focus one's attention on a slender steel pole that's nine stories tall. It reminded me of the Maypole, although I've never actually seen one.

Five *Volantes* begin with a ceremony at the base of the steel pole. They circle the pole in a ritualistic dance led by a flute player. I was told that they are asking the gods for blessings. Then they climb the pole that has a small, square frame at the very top. The square reminded me of *Ojo de Díos* (Eye of God), the colorful diamond squares ones sees in Mexico.

The climb itself is rigorous and physically demanding. Four *Volantes* arrange themselves, sitting on the rails of the open frame.

The fifth member of the *Volantes,* the last to climb, mounts the very apex of the pole where he dances and plays a flute. His dance floor must be less than a foot square and there he taps his feet in rhythm, oblivious apparently to the dizzying height.

The four *Volantes* represent the cardinal points, north, south, east and west. Seated on the edge of the frame, the four, each and together, slowly turn the platform frame like a giant clockwork and wind the yellow cord around the pole until all the slack is taken up.

Each *Volante* ties a cord to his waist and wraps it around an ankle. At a given moment, in unison, all four fall backwards with arms extended. In falling, they spin like upside-down whirling dervishes in ecstasy. Each circles the pole thirteen times as he glides to earth, symbolically bringing the sun and the rain to the Mother Earth to nurture seeds that bring life and fertility. This is a rite that was once widespread before the arrival of the Spaniards. It is maintained by the Tononacs and now brings in a shower of coins from the tourists.

The age range of the *Volantes* surprised me. While most are young men, some are novices of thirteen years old while others could be grandfathers. I suspect that it's the grueling climb up the pole that encourages retirement.

Before I left, I asked the *Volantes* if I could take a group photo.

 "¿Como no? (Of course)," was the friendly answer. I was not the only tourist with a camera, but when the others had taken their pictures and left, I asked, "Can you tell me about your decorative outfit?"

A *Volante* was happy to explain, "We used to dress as bird-men, that's what our history says, but the Spanish priests prohibited it as pagan. So we designed fancy clothes and said that it was a game."

He explained that on the headdress, a comb made of multicolored folds represented the rainbow; the mirrors, the sun; flowers on the cap, growth of vegetation. The long streamers I guessed represented the rain, but no, they represented corn, the agricultural staple of the Mexican diet. The streamers were symbolic corn tassels.

From the center I still had a five-minute walk to the *colectivo* stand. When I arrived, the driver told me to sit up front. I was alone and as soon as I got in, we were off to Playa del Carmen.

Playa del Carmen is the ultimate tourist beachfront shopping bazaar. I enjoyed the utter overexposure to Mexican shopping and brand name luxury businesses. I paid $6 for a scoop of Häagen Dazs Pralines and Cream with a special dipped cone. Starbucks was prominent as were Carlos and Charlie's, too. Luxury shops line Calle Cinco (Fifth Street) and there is enough electricity glowing in the jewelry stores to power most hotels.

Expenses: Taxi & combi $18, bus $10, meals $18, Hotel La Ziranda $44, fees $18, Total: $108.

DAY 38
Leaving: Playa del Carmen and the Cancun Airport

Bus Journey across Mexico

On Playa del Carmen's Fifth Street, the beach town's shopping heart, next to the tourist shop paying homage to Frida Kahlo, I found an efficient travel agent handling incoming calls and simultaneously punching up airline schedules on the computer. I asked to purchase a ticket for Mexico City. He recommended Click Airlines. "It's part of Mexicana, but like United's Ted, it's the economical service," he said.

Click had an early flight. That suited me. I like early mornings in Mexico. I was up, packed and ready by 5 a.m. Hotel la Ziranda was only two blocks from the bus depot, but the airport bus wouldn't leave until 7 a.m.

I had saved money on Click, but I'd have to spend the savings on a taxi.

I loaded myself down with three bags and walked to the corner, down the street from my hotel. It was dark, misty and quiet. I stood at the corner. Immediately a cab flashed its lights. I waved. "How much to Cancun Airport?"

The driver pulled out a rate card, "$40," he said. The $5 and $10 hourly rates I had earlier been offered on my trip were not available here.

We negotiated. I said, "Its early, no traffic, it's a 30-minute ride, round trip, you'll be back in an hour. You might get a fare back."

We agreed to $30. I put my bags in the back seat, sat down in the front seat and chatted. Along the highway there were huge stonewalls with gated entryways to new resorts under construction. The driver pointed out three new hotels, "All Spanish," he said.

I thought, how ironic. When I was in Spain in the sixties, Spain was poor and selling its beaches to Germans and Scandinavians. Now Spaniards are buying Mexico's beaches.

It was a quick ride. Light was dawning. The airport was silent. I was early and check-in was fast. I was on my way home.

Expenses: Taxi $30

"Taxi $30" was the last entry in my epic journal, which covered only the highlights, I felt like Marco Polo telling a story of adventure and discovery, yet still leaving out so very much.

Going Home: Thoughts

On the plane home I grabbed a window seat, buckled in, felt and heard the swoosh of the airplane's acceleration. Peering out of the window I watched the flat Yucatan grow small as the plane lifted high. Eager to return home, I recalled the concerns my friends and family had about my safety traveling alone, busing across Mexico. But for thirty-eight days I'd been welcomed countless times, treated cordially, often thoughtfully when seeking directions, asking about hotels or inquiring at tourist offices. I wasn't special and my well-being never seemed to be in doubt.

As I reflected, I thought of adding some encouragement to the independent traveler who might consider Mexico a destination, away from the beaches and resorts, to venture into a mosaic of discovery, to take the opportunity to realize a cultural quest, to experience Mexico's music, art, crafts, architecture, to learn another language, study a history apart from our own and a pre-history unlike any other. I'd written articles on Mexico and recommended books, which were meant to inform and educate. These I decided to add as a postscript. Here follows a short Spanish lesson hoping to kick-start an adventure and a variety of commentaries meant to inform visitors and travelers with the hope that some might be inspired to take the bus from Tijuana to Chetumal.

So you want to learn **Spanish?** Here's a start!

Don's Amazing Anyone-Can-Speak-Spanish Method

My friend Don was a can-do, persistent guy, but on a scale of one to ten for Spanish Aptitude, Don rated a minus three. The Marines created his can-do attitude by teaching Don that all obstacles were surmountable inconveniences. His persistence got him into a Spanish mess.

In 1963 Don fell in love with a Mexican girl, the hotel owner's daughter whom he met in Guaymas on the Sea of Cortez while fishing. During this short romance, Don learned a few phases and cordial greetings, "Mi casa es su casa," most of the items on a Mexican menu, road signs like "tope" which means "speed bump," and other basics. But most of all he learned that he liked Mexican girls.

Later, he got a job in Mexico City with a real estate development firm selling condos to Americans. But he couldn't put a Spanish sentence together. Conjugation, masculine and feminine nouns requiring adjectives to agree with gender, just wouldn't stick. He studied Spanish, took a private one-on-one course, and drove the instructor nuts, or as Don said, "bananas."

Then it clicked. He invented Don's Amazing Anyone-Can-Speak Spanish Method. Courtesy and infinitives were parts of the secret formula. Don learned, "Perdóneme," (excuse me), "Usted es muy amable," (you are very kind), "Usted es muy simpático," (you are very nice). He would compliment a child, "Muy guapa," (very pretty) or "muy guapo," (very handsome). Parents would smile, nod approval, and say, "Grácias, Señor."

Don could keep a half-understood conversation going by looking interested and asking, "Y por qué?" (And why was that?). He played dominos in the bars, slapped the tiles down like a Cuban, and when one of the players added his piece to the game, Don would look intense, and say "Por qué?" as if he were calculating the odds of the remaining pieces outstanding and thoroughly intimidate everyone at the table.

But his real coup de language was "es possible?" (Is it possible?) plus an infinitive. "Es posible?" plus an infinitive gave Don a leg up on a language. All those conjugations were put on hold. Don was a pragmatic, can-do, and get-it-done guy. He believed, "Marines do the job; others made it look nice." So he memorized infinitives, added "es posible?" and spoke Spanish. Sometimes he stuck a noun after "es posible?" as circumstance required, and later he added "es necesario?" (is it necessary?) to his amazing method.

Don would travel and ask at the hotel desk, "Es posible dormir? (to sleep) and even if the clerk spoke some English, he'd answer Don in Spanish. Don usually got the idea, the room number, the amount, and when the price was mentioned, he'd say "Por qué?" with a face requesting a discount. In a cantina Don would brightly say, "Es posible tomar (to drink) una cerveza (a beer)?" At a restaurant he began, "Es posible comer (to eat)?"

Pagar (to pay), ir (to go), venir (to come), encontrar, (to find), salir (to leave), usar (to use), were parts of Don's vocabulary. When he spoke at length, he sounded like Jeff Chandler playing the part of Cochise in an old western cavalry movie, clipping the jargon but getting the job done.

On a trip to Mexico, Don took me sightseeing. Frequently, Don asked directions, "Perdóneme, es posible, Taxco?" (Taxco: a colonial silver town east of Mexico City). A woman walking barefoot, carrying a bundle, pointed the way, speaking, "Allá, allá, (that way)." Don replied, "Usted es muy amable." She smiled and nodded her head. We traveled and shopped. Don bargained. At a bar in Zacatecas, Don asked, "Es posible música (music)?" And we got a nine-member Mariachi band to play at our table. They were also "Muy amable."

Don never conquered Spanish grammar. Word-to-word memorization added to his vocabulary and understanding. He appreciated most conversations and watched the Mexican soap operas. "There are only six occupations in Mexico," he said "doctor, lawyer, engineer, gardener, maid, and mistress." He got the sense of most newspaper headlines but relied on "The News," a Mexican paper printed in English for expats.

Don died in 1994. He lived in Mexico for over twenty years, married, and raised a family. I like to think that when Don knocked on the Pearly Gates, he asked, "Perdónme, es posible entrar?" And St. Peter indicating, "Come in," replied, "Usted es muy amable."

Don't know much about history? Mexican Street Maps To the Rescue!

I was in San Luis Potosi attending a lecture at the Casa Cultura when it occurred to me that I could learn a great deal of history, the history that's important to the average Mexican, the milestones that a Mexican feels in his heart, from street signs.

I had just walked down Calle Marzo 18 (March 18th Street) and curious about that name, I asked the man seated next to me in the lecture room. He was elderly, well dressed, distinguished and courteous in a manner that one rarely finds today. He said, "March 18, 1938, was when Larzaro Cardenas, President of Mexico expropriated the oil." He explained that although Mexico was suffering a depression in 1938 and seemed to be in the grips of foreign oil companies, the nation responded en mass by donating money, jewels and precious belonging to pay for the expropriation. "Peasants brought in chickens."

Even today, Mexicans deeply feel a near-sacred belief about ownership of their oil reserves and the Mexican national monopoly Pemex. This feeling is surpassed only by the commitment Mexicans attach to Tonatzin, the Virgin of Guadalupe, who is more than an icon. "Even atheists venerate Guadalupe," a guide told me, "and her shrine and sanctuary were respected even by those who shot priests during the Cristeros War."

Many streets and avenues are named for heroes and commemorate dates. Cinco de Mayo (May 5), the day the Mexican army defeated the French invaders in the Battle of Puebla, is a popular street name throughout Mexico.

Doce de Diciembre (December 12) is the day Juan Diego, a convert to Catholicism, who had a vision of the Virgin of Guadalupe, presented proof of this miracle, unrolling his tilma (cloak) before the Bishop of Mexico and finding the picture of the Virgin which is venerated and on display in Mexico City at the church of the Virgin of Guadalupe.

There is 16 de Septiembe, Independence Day, 22 de Noviembre, the start of the Revolution that is a virtual holiday in honor of Pancho Villa.

For a snapshot of the important events in Mexico's history, get a city map and look over the index, or when you're walking, note the streets and avenues that are named for a date. Then when you visit a cyber café to check your email, take a moment, use a search engine and type in: Mexico History, the date and the month, and learn while you travel.

Mexican Holidays

All towns and states celebrate local heroes, Saints Days and hold fairs, which may be an exposition of art, crafts, music or books. Pagentry, processions and performances in the plazas are so common that I take them for granted.

National Holidays

1 January – New Year's Day
6 January- Three Kings' Day
5 February –Constitution Day
21 March – Benito Juarez Birthday
Maundy Thursday – Thursday before Easter Sunday
Good Friday - Friday before Easter Sunday
Easter Sunday
1 May – Labor Day
5 May – Battle of Puebla

16 September – Mexican Independence Day
1 November–2 - Day of the Dead
20 November -Revolution
12 December - Our Lady of Guadalupe Day
24 December – Christmas Eve
25 December – Christmas Day

Music, Melodies, Mariachis

Friends ask, "What do you like about Mexico?"

I begin with food, not fancy, but meals I enjoy. "I like beans and rice, enchiladas and tacos and a cold beer. I could live on guacamole and totopos (chips)." I love simple family restaurants and ice cream parlors that are so wildly painted in bright colors that they make the rainbow look pallid.

I like the outdoor markets, the handcrafts, the colorful pottery from the town of Dolores Hidalgo, and the tiles from Puebla. I like macabre masks and The Day of the Dead. I love the Cervantino, the three-week festival that celebrates Miguel Cervantes and performs his short comic plays. It's held annually in Guanajuato.

I love the pageantry, the parades and processions, the fairs, the colonial buildings, the abandoned and the renovated haciendas, the former convents that may now be a hotel, a museum or a restaurant, tours of old mines, Diego Rivera Murals and the surprises that tell me, "You're not in Kansas anymore."

I don't care about the beaches.

I like temples and pyramids and excavations and the mysteries of lost civilizations. I like the history of the Spanish Conquest and following historic routes. I've visited the homes of Cortes, Zapata, Pancho Villa, Benito Juarez and Santa Ana. And I've tracked down migrant workers in the U.S. back to their village and homes in the Sierra Madre Mountains.

Mexico is history and adventure. It's loud and brazen. It's colorful and mysterious. It's about people and their charm. It's not without frustration or misunderstandings. You learn about yourself as you gain an understanding of Mexican's culture. I don't think there is another national border that you can cross from one country to the next and sense such a radical change.

Above all, Mexico to me is music. I love mariachis and their songs, their corridos, ballads, and rancheras. I enjoy José Alfredo Jimenez, Lola Beltrán and Paquita del Barrio, songs of the Revolution, love songs, songs of heroes, songs of distress and songs that encapsulate history and protest injustice.

There is vitality in Mexican music, and it's everywhere. Musicians in bars, on the bus, in restaurants, on the street, in the plazas, all offer their services. I've hired mariachis in groups of nine, wearing charro outfits, as well as conjuntos (five-member bands) dressed in white, and even a lone guitarist, Ricardo Reys, in Boca Grande, who asked a few questions and then made up "my song" on the spot.

I'm pleased with marimbas in Veracruz, and I can listen to a fellow with a violin joined with a guitarist. They come singly and in bands. There are Tunas, student clubs dressed in Spanish costume. They stroll in and out of restaurants and play romantic ballads. You'll find musicians wheeling harps down the street, looking for a customer. There is chamber music and street music. Mexico is a land of musical joy and often has a deeper meaning.

Corridos, Mexican ballads, are a source of history. Songs are "oral newspapers." They often tell you about the time and place of an event and highlight a hero defending his rights. Sometimes the hero is infamous, as in the current batch of Narco Corridos.

I first noticed this when I bought a Cancionero, a Mexican songbook. I wanted to read *"La Cucaracha,"* especially the part about the cockroach who ran out of marijuana.

I learned a couple of things: *"La Cucaracha"* refers to a "camp follower," and she sells everything, yep, that's one story. Then another told me that, "La Cucaracha is Huerta" the dictator who's unclean in his habits and who also smoked the weed.

That was fun to read, although questionable in scholarship. But I did learn from *"La Cucaracha"* that sarapes come from Satillo, real men from Chihuahua, and the best looking gals from Jalisco.

Further along in the songbook, it seemed like every town in Mexico had a hero and recorded the news in a corrido. I read the lyrics to *"La Persecución de Villa,"* which told about Pancho Villa's escape from Black Jack Pershing with the Americans in pursuit. Reading the story, read like a journalist's report.

But Professor James "Big Jim" Griffith, folklorist in Tucson, Arizona, corrected my perceptions. "Corridos are more than news, they are editorials, and they express opinions." He's right, of course. They are emotional and one-sided in their viewpoint. We would not consider Pancho's raid on Columbus, New Mexico, heroic, but the corrido presented a story like David and Goliath, and the fact was Pancho got away.

I called Big Jim because I was interested in knowing whether Mexico had cowboy songs, and he was an expert. He collected corridos from the Arizona-Sonoran borderlands and published a CD, *"Heroes and Horses."* Big Jim said, "Mexico does not have an exact parallel to American cowboy songs, but songs about horses and horse races are close." He told me the story about El Moro (Dapple Grey) and Rélampago (Lightning) and their match race held March 17, 1957, in Agua Prieta that's celebrated in song. The grand event is one of the corridos recorded on *"Heroes and Horses."*

He said that corridos are often about heroes standing alone, brave men, facing each other, "pecho a pecho" like two roosters squaring off, chest to chest. The heroes are idealized, and the social fabric is on display.

301

His comments reminded me of Gary Cooper in the movie *High Noon*, one man standing alone. I asked him how the social fabric was expressed. He said, for example, that while all the horses are praised, and their riders honored (even the losers as long as they showed themselves to be worthy), there is a group of songs, generally about the owners, who are condemned for chicanery, dishonesty, and trickery.

When musicians offer to play, I'll be asking, "How about playing your favorite corrido?" I'm interested in the culture, the heroes, the history and the music, music, music.

Safe Travel in Mexico

In April 2009, David Kaufman, International Travel Editor, *American Express Magazine*, asked me for my opinion about the negative publicity concerning drugs and violence Mexico. Here is my reply.

"As an inveterate traveler for over a decade, I have found a great deal of pleasure and adventure searching historic Mexico. I don't know much about beaches and beer but I've retraced the footsteps of Miguel Hidalgo, Emiliano Zapata, Pancho Villa, Hernán Cortés, Santa Ana, Benito Juarez, Francisco Madero and Venustiano Carranza and ventured into many colonial cities and remote places.

I can't directly say how Mexico is dealing with the negative press on the drug trade, but in my personal experience, I believe it's akin to being in Chicago in the 1920s. No one has bothered me in tens of thousands of miles traveling across Mexico by bus and in my Grand Marquis. I don't seek out drugs or look for "speakeasies." I use common sense. When I've been told not to go some place, I've mostly taken the advice. I travel with a belief that caution, secure parking and mild paranoia are apt to keep the traveler safe, not only in Mexico but in all foreign and domestic adventures.

I've had misadventures, if one calls flat tires or having the Grand Marquis stuck off the road in remote places or arriving after midnight when something went wrong. I've rarely made a hotel reservation in advance, and always people have been helpful and kind. I haven't been stupid or naive when I've had problems.

But I think the most important factor is not the place but the person. Teenagers on Spring break can open doors to tragedy anywhere. Late nights in strange places and drugs or binge drinking, well that's not safe conduct anywhere. Tourists sometimes let their hair down and don't watch their wallet. That's not wise, ever, on any trip.

I've read about the narco-wars, and of course when police, politicians and military officers have been assassinated, I've paid attention. Kidnappings I've also read about. Profession or wealth marks these unfortunate people. But why would anyone kidnap a random tourist? Or take a shot at a traveler?

I would not hang around the border towns. One glimpse is enough. But I wouldn't hesitate to spend an evening in Zacatecas, join a callejonera winding through the ancient streets in company with a donkey and dance with the entourage.

In essence, I believe I'm as safe on the road traveling in Mexico as in the U.S."

Shopping in Mexico

I hadn't thought about it, I mean about all the Mexican treasures that decorate my home. It was my granddaughter Isabela who mentioned it. Well, she didn't exactly mention it to me, she told her teacher.

They were studying the family in second grade (you know how important it is to build values), and the teacher asked the students to write what they liked about visiting their grandparents.

Isabela wrote, "I really love my grandpa because he has a lot of Mexican art." She also mentioned our trips for ice cream and wrote that she liked to visit grandma 'cause grandma lets her watch television. That's another topic, but as for her interest in my decorations, I wasn't even aware that she had noticed.

My taste runs to bright and colorful. Folk art, handcrafts, masks, ceramics that gleam with swirls of color: these are items I enjoy. And my second grader likes them too.

So I'm in Mexico, in Puebla, a beautiful colonial city south of Mexico City on the way to Veracruz. I'm rummaging around the Plaza de los Sapos, where they have the weekend antique and flea market, and it's jammed. As I pick up some old piece of iron that looks like a lion head doorknocker, I start thinking about where I purchased all those things that Isabela likes and where I'd recommend a traveler shop.

I've bought pottery directly from the artisans in Mata Ortiz. The whole town has prospered because Juan Quezada revived Paquimé-styled pots. But buying from the maker and getting a picture really makes the piece special. Mata Ortiz is in Northern Mexico, Chihuahua, near Casas Grandes and the pots, decorated, geometrically stylized, are beautiful.

I've purchased silver items, silver angels and a pitcher shaped like a duck where the beak is the spout, from the Castillos. They're a family of silversmiths who have their shop just outside of Taxco. It's a short ride in a taxi, but you get a tour of the workshop and see craftsmen at work.

In Tonala, it's now part of Guadalajara, I once asked the local tourist office if I could see how papier-mâché was made, and I got a personal introduction and guided tour. I also got a large green and yellow parrot that swings overhead in my dining room. I never have to feed it, and it never makes a mess. I'll have to ask Isabela if she likes my bird.

I've purchased Huichol masks from street venders in Real de Catorce. They're made of wood, slathered in beeswax then covered bead by tiny bead in multiple rainbow colors to make symbolic designs. If you look, you can find styalized corn, deer, eagles and scorpions. Peyote blossoms are frequent and some are right in the mask's center, on the nose. The one I kept is a real beauty. It's special to me because I've never seen another female

Huichol mask.

Sometimes I find things in unexpected places, like a basket I bought in a restaurant or the time I purchased a painting and a charcoal drawing right off the wall from a small coffee shop in Dolores Hidalgo. Somehow I treasure the item more when it's not from a store. But you have to be lucky. I even traded a baseball bat for a black pot in Mata Ortiz. I didn't want the pot. Black is not my favorite color, but the kid wanted my bat, and we made a deal. Now that little black pot is a treasure chest.

My treasures are personal. Yours will be too.

But if you're on your way to Mexico, and you like Mexican traditions, folk crafts that are bright and beautiful, and don't have time to get lucky, here's what I advise. The three best shopping places, the most consistent for superior quality and variety, that I've found are at museum shops, Sanborns and the Casa de Artesanias, sometimes called Casa de Artesanos, sponsored by Fonart (Fondo Nacional para el Formento de las Artesanias). The government runs these shops with an eye on keeping the best craftsmen working.

Oaxaca: The Weaver's Art Simply Complex

The pre-Hispanic ruins at the Mitla Temple Complex in Oaxaca, Mexico reveal a direct connection to the modern Zapotec weaver's art. Mitla's tall-walled avenue, sculptured in bas-relief, dwarfs the visitor. Three broad bands of geometric mosaic designs, pieced together in polished stones, contain the lasting record of encoded knowledge and a glimpse into Zapotec beliefs. Repeating patterns from the past are preserved in the threads woven by modern artisans whose textiles preserve and celebrate Zapotec beliefs. Ironically, Mitla, Place of the Dead, is alive in the carpets of the living.

Along the avenue in Mitla, the lower band on the wall is the sacred calendrical lightning design. The middle shows the greca, the four steps of life: birth, childhood, youth and maturity. Zapotecs believe grecas link all forms of life together. The top band is composed of stylized geometric caracols (snails) that symbolize the continuation of life.

Figures and symbols, neglected for hundreds of years, relics from destroyed temples, are features in Oaxacan carpets. Weavers follow tradition without full knowledge of their origin or significance. Investigators have speculated that patterns, stylized feathers and scales, birds and snakes, may symbolize the energy of the sky and the shaking of the earth and represent the duality of the body and spirit interlocked in the pan-Mexican icon Quetzalcoatl, the Feathered Serpent.

Zenon Hipolito, a master weaver born in 1956 in Teotitlan del Valle, Oaxaca, lives with his family in a modern ranch-styled home. He has three treadle looms in the living room, which seems a perfect symbolic melding of the modern with the ancient art. To explain the loom, he showed me a sketch and labeled the parts in combined English, Spanish and Zapotec.

His treasure is a carpet, woven by his father Ponciano, a traditional black-red, two-color design with a flower center. Zapotec weavers once used only the black-red combination, but over time, with collectors and tourists, art and use influenced color. Carpets became wall hangings.

The flower at the center of the treasured carpet symbolizes nourishment. "We honor the flower because it represents food." The bloom of the calabaza (squash) is a Zapotec favorite. The colors are symbolic. Red represents the sun or day; black the night, but the dichotomy may also extend to male-female, good-evil, vitality-rest. Secret recipes for vegetable dye colors are passed from generation to generation, and like Napa Valley vintners, one family can identify another's work by subtle differences. "We can tell right away."

Zenon Hipolito crafted his own looms, the largest being ten feet wide. He brings a portable 4x4-foot loom to art fairs and demonstrates his craft, which requires constant attention to the mathematics of the design. Geometric figures are complex, but the curved figures, whether a bird or flower or sun or moon or animal image, are the most difficult to weave and likely to be least appreciated by the casual viewer. "When did you begin weaving? I asked Zenon.

"When I was eight," he said. His father, a master weaver, taught him, and Zenon had to learn the most difficult designs first, the curves.

"How often do we challenge the student with the hardest first," I wondered? Zenon's eyes gleamed, and his Mona Lisa smile turned radiant when he spoke of his father, who died in 2008.

"The best yarn comes from Chichicapan, a town near Oaxaca. They raise their own sheep and have the best handspun wool." Sheep and goat wool is used in its natural color or is naturally dyed in earth tones. A bluestone is ground to make indigo; yellow comes from the onion, green from the pepper tree, and walnuts or pecans provide brown. The cochineal insect is dried and ground to create a deep red.

One may see a cruciform and think of the cross, but it's a compass indicating cardinal points and the elements of life: earth, sun, water and air. Browns and grays are earth colors. Reds and yellows honor the life-giving sun. Blues and green represent water and white air. Zenon showed me a carpet with the sun at the center, which was composed of four elements and colors. I was thinking phases of the moon and sun. "The moon is in eclipse," he said. But a sliver shadowing the crescent moon was a deeper blue. "Every time my mother saw an eclipse, she put water outside to relieve the sun." This personal experience became part of the carpet.

A carpet may use any number of aesthetic elements, stylized geometric figures, offsetting adjacent colors and negative-positive images created by designs. "The butterfly represents long-lasting life and the caracol (snail, stylized spiral) we believe continues life; your culture goes on and on and on. The center is energy, our belly button, Mother Earth." Patterns of four repeat, as there are four steps in life. Checkerboard crosses using squares and triangles symbolized the life force and energy. The cloud motif, a symmetrical pattern of small squares arranged from the center point of the cloud in a six-to-four-to-two ratio is a sign of plenty and an abundant harvest. Repeating triangles in an arrow pattern, stylized scales or feathers, are signs of long life and energy. Butterflies, geometric Xs or threes back-to-back are also longevity symbols. The lightning pattern contains sacred calendrical signs. Squares and diamonds incorporate contrasting elements often using colors, arrows and shading. Some symbolize God's eyes and insight into the future.

Historically, weavers did not sign their carpets, but collectors have made that request so some weavers are encoding their birthdate into their newest designs, since the date of birth once was a Zapotec's given name.

Day of the Dead
An Insider's View of San Miguel de Allende

Once a year, St. Paul's Episcopal Church in San Miguel de Allende offers an opportunity to enjoy an insider's view of San Miguel de Allende, stay with a family, mix with expats, see how they live, learn why they chose San Miguel, and participate in a major Mexican tradition: The Day of the Dead. It's the major fundraiser of the year for Feed the Hungry, a charitable program, and most of the cost of the tour goes to support a school lunch program for impoverished Mexican children.

I generally believe the word "tour" is anathema to the independent traveler. But with my daughter Nena and granddaughter Isabela, I took a risk, and signed up.

We embarked on St. Paul's seven-day, six-night Day of the Dead tour. It felt like a holiday, where we spent time with friends and attended events. We were never rushed or bused around. We were scattered around town in private homes, yet not far from the center, and our hosts, graciously offering us a key to their homes, made us feel like visiting family. Most events were within walking distance.

Days went by quickly. The first morning, the sun came up with a golden brilliance. I went out in the crisp, fresh air and vacant streets for a vigorous hike. From my street, I could see the morning sun silhouetting a cross at the top of the hill. I grabbed my camera and headed east. I huffed and puffed; with each step the street seemed to rise vertically like Taylor in San Francisco. At 6500 feet, you get winded quickly, but what a view of San Miguel in the sun's first light. Shadows cupped San Miguel while the gothic church, the centerpiece of the city, mirrored the sun's glory.

After breakfast with our respective host family, we took a walking tour of San Miguel de Allende. We started at the Episcopal Church, which is just a block from Instituto Allende. The Instituto, a refurbished country estate once owned by the Count of Canal, is now an art, photography and language school founded by Stirling Dickenson and friends. The building is a colonial beauty, with arches, colonnades, patios and a terrace restaurant. It has one of the best views of downtown San Miguel. Stirling's Instituto Allende and the Bellas Artes School were the original magnets for the expat community that is currently estimated at 11,000 full- and part-time residents. You don't have to speak much Spanish to enjoy San Miguel de Allende.

We visited La Parroquia, the magnificent Gothic church that I saw in the morning sunlight. It was designed and constructed by Zeferino Gutierrez, an indigenous master builder, who was inspired by a Gothic church pictured in a postcard. Our timing was perfect. A just-married bride and groom came out of the church flanked by friends, family and a mariachi band. A horse and carriage awaited the newlyweds then carried them off like Cinderella and the Prince.

We crossed the main plaza, the Jardín, in front of La Parroquia, and stopped for lunch at Bellas Artes. We passed by beautiful shops on Calle Zacateras, visited the Mercado and bought Day of the Dead sugar skulls. San Miguel de Allende offers the best in folk art, crafts, carvings, woodwork, fine art, textiles, leather, silver, and Talavera pottery. But we only took time to peek. We saved our time for real shopping later.

The original expats, in late 1940s and early 1950s, were young, Bohemian and often students living on the GI Bill. But the expats I met or saw on the streets, in the cafés and markets were of retirement age. They have basically created their own separate society with an active calendar. Scottsdale South, I called it. I was curious why the current expat retirees chose San Miguel.

"The climate," was the instant answer. I got the feeling that I wasn't the first to ask, and the expats had agreed on this two-word answer. Low real estate taxes and cost of living would sound unglamorous. Some answered in three words, "Sunshine and culture."

Art is the central activity. Dining and friendly conversation at Pegaso Café must also rank highly. The Instituto Allende offers painting, photography and sculpture. One of our hosts designs clothes and owns an elegant shop. When my daughter and I dropped into El Tecolote (The Owl) bookstore looking for books in Spanish, the more prominently displayed English books were on: art, garden and cooking.

Cami Sands gave me a more complete answer. "We love the weather, scenery, the compact town, the style of 'inward houses,' the arts, restaurants and the friendliness of the Americans who live here." She also mentioned, "Our ability to impact good works via church, Rotary and other charities," and concluded, "We like the Mexican people, their celebrations, their love of children."

I spoke to Rosalia, a Mexican lady, who said there once was some resentment, but that Mexicans are good hosts and the Americans have proved to be good guests. She said, "They have brought in capital, and they support the community with charitable works. Expats have caused prices to rise, but have brought employment." Saturday evening we attended a before-dinner fiesta, a musician entertained and hors d'oeuvres were served in the home of a working artist. Floor-by-floor we found ourselves admiring the antiques, the paintings, the gardens, a pool and on the fourth floor, a terrace with the artist's studio, with a mirador overlooking San Miguel de Allende.

We went to church twice on Sunday, Catholic and Episcopal, Spanish and English. After the Episcopal service, we boarded a bus for a short ride to the Rev. Harold Weicker's hacienda, which in itself is a religious art museum. Here we enjoyed the hacienda party, with mariachis and San Miguel's famous carnival giant puppets.

Monday was our busy day. As previously mentioned, we toured the primary school, saw the lunch program in action and spoke with the teachers and the bright-eyed, energetic children. The kids entertained us, and the church at Atotonilco surprised us.

The church, founded in 1740, is painted with Michelangelo-like virtuosity and is listed as a UNESCO World Heritage site. Indigenous artists painted the church's dramatically themed interior: the life, passion and resurrection of Christ. It was from this Jesuit sanctuary that Father Miguel Hidalgo took the banner of Guadalupe and led the Mexican insurgents against the Spanish in the War of Independence.

From the village of Atotonilco, we departed for a late lunch at Rancho Jaguar hosted by Robert and Jennifer Haas. Jennifer started collecting Mexican folk art in 1966, and the collection grew over the years. Rancho Jaguar now devotes a private museum to this collection.

Tuesday, a day of leisure, we looked around the shops and art galleries. That evening, we were guests at a patio-garden dinner and Day of the Dead altar ceremony. Many of us brought pictures of a departed friend or family member we wished to honor. We placed it on the ofrenda (offering) altar among the marigold flowers.

Marigolds, with their heady fragrance, copal (incense) and candles are said to guide souls back to this once-a-year reunion with the living. To me, the altar honored the dead and celebrated life and the life to come by being aware and not afraid of the transition named "Death." In anticipation of a visiting soul, altars are decorated with the loved one's favorite food, drink (typically tequila), cigarettes, mementos and always pan de muerto, a special round loaf of bread.

Maria Teresa, a Tarahumara shaman, led the ritual and explained Catholic-Indian tradition. The four elements were represented: Earth as fruits and vegetables, Air as papel picada (tissue paper), Fire as candles, and Water. Flowers signified eternal life with God. Candles lit the way for the soul's return. Water, symbol of purity, also quenched the soul's thirst. Copal cleansed the area from bad spirits. Pan de muerto represented the bodies of the departed.

Wednesday we were free until 2 p.m. We then met in St. Paul's Hall for a lecture by Fred Stresen-Reuter, an historian, who gave us a detailed and informative lecture on the similarities of Catholicism and Aztec beliefs and how they melded in the Day of the Dead ceremony.

After his presentation, we walked to the Panteón, San Miguel's cemetery, which was festooned with a field of flowers. Graves were decorated with golden marigolds, as our altar had been the previous evening. It was a time of joy and sadness.

Later that evening we gathered for our farewell dinner. Troubadours in 16th-century costume, a "tuna" in Spanish, entertained us outdoors in the patio-garden, under the veranda.

For information about next year's Inside San Miguel de Allende, email: contact@feedthehungrysma.org

Teaching English in Mexico as a Volunteer

Although I have a California teaching credential, and taught finance and English for the Cross Cultural Institute in San Luis

Potosi, I earned a diploma to Teaching English as a Second Language and then joined Global Volunteers. I spent three months in Mexico, teaching in both Queretaro and Dolores Hidalgo. I went early to enjoy the Cervantino, an international music-theater-dance festival held annually in Guanajuato. Here are my comments, thoughts, reflections, opinions and exaggerations from that experience.

From the journal

Mexico is an unfulfilled land of promise, the frustration of hope, the girl with the beautiful smile and bright eyes who was forced to drop out and help support her family, a nation that was intellectually renowned on the world stage in the 19th century with the Cientificos, whose beauty glows in the past colonial splendor, the Porfirio Diaz dominated era and the School of Muralists.

I signed up to teach English to "the future workers of America," in central Mexico for the fall. I started driving from Alameda, California, and I took a long route, going north and east so I could visit my mother and family before disappearing into the Mexican desert.

The border crossing took close to an hour in a nearly empty building with only two people ahead of me in line. No one inspected my car or asked for the removal of luggage, which could add to the hassle. Time just was of no concern.

My first destination was Guanajuato, Mexico, where the annual Cervantino Festival brings international artists, musicians, dancers, yet mainly Mexican tourists. Hotel Parador San Javier, a beautiful place, gave me a quiet room with a super-sized bed. Two people could turn out the lights and never find one another the whole night. Maybe I wasn't alone!

I hoofed it all over Guanajuato's cobblestone streets, through the tunnels, up to the Pipila monument that overlooks the town, wove my way through the labyrinth of crooked streets that frequently opened into sunlit patios often festooned with flowers. I wore out my legs, found a few muscles I had forgotten about. I bought tickets to four events, but the major outdoor show each night at the Alhondiga, was free. To the surprise of everyone in this T-shirt climate, unseasonable cold weather brought thunder, lightning and showers, which had the audience sporting umbrellas during sporadic downpours the first two nights. Crowds were thinned, sponsors disappointed.

This year, music of Veracruz, its Caribbean origins, sea shanties, and its famous composer Augustin Lara, set the musical theme. Fifty harps, the perfect instrument for angels, crowded the stage under cover, fearing rain, leaving less room for the dance numbers.

I took an exciting hike into the nearby and newly opened, Ecological Zone, where the local guide was occupied with a group picnic as I ventured into the wilds alone. After a while all trees, shrubs, paths looked the same. I used my Sunday comic-strip memory of Mark Trail and his outdoor wisdom to mark my path with stones as I ventured into the wilderness.

If laughter is the measuring stick, the most fun I had was watching two street mimes, identical twin brothers, performing, clowning, satirizing and pulling the public audience into their routines.

After Guanajuato, I drove south to Queretaro to join the Global Volunteers. We stayed at Hotel El Señorial, which enjoys a perfect location on the edge of the protected colonial heritage zone. Volunteers found that recruitment literature had failed to mention "indentured servitude" or "slavery," which I quickly learned to be the case. No one complained, but we were scheduled to work a six-day week, classes beginning at 7 a.m. Each day began in pitch darkness, 5:50 a.m., without breakfast because not even the underpaid kitchen staff began before 7.

Our school van picked us up at 6:30 for the twenty-minute ride to the university where we participated in five straight classes before lunch, then two after, and a return to the hotel at 4 p.m. Breakfast became a daily banana and a cup of school coffee. School lunches were only so-so, and I preferred "Cup of Noodles." So my friend

Everett was on the mark when I told him about volunteering to teach and he had said, "Davis, have you been taking dumb pills?"

Queretaro is far different from my memory of fifteen-or-so years ago. There was no beauty then that I recall. What sticks in my mind is that the bandstand was so dilapidated that the musicians used care arranging their chairs so as not to fall through the floor, and it was not a minor inconvenience. Today the entire colonial center (at least a half-mile square) has been refurbished. It is well-tended, pedestrian friendly, attractive with well-maintained plazas with delightful, artistic, fountains, outdoor cafés, a wide variety of restaurants, bookstores, coffee shops, and music everywhere. I now put Queretero at the top of my Mexican list.

The English classes were basic. Most students had just one semester under their belt. The Mexican teachers used us for conversation, primed the students to ask, "What is your name, where are you from, do you like tequila, what is your favorite Mexican food, do you like Mexico, do you have children, etc." This repetition allowed me to create and repeat the same jokes.

I explained "Dick" is a nickname of Richard, similar to Francisco-Pancho, which I elaborated with some positive comment about Pancho Villa, who Mexicans, especially the youth, view as a hero for his raid on Columbus, New Mexico. They take pride in our subsequent failure to bring him to justice in 1916.

Mexicans have little sympathy for the U.S. They view us as the Great El Norte Bully, who stole their land, invaded their territory, scorned and pushed them around. They note every dogfight with us as some David-versus-Goliath unresolved injustice. Well, it's justice when we get the bloody nose, like Pancho's raid, or kicking out the oil companies in 1938. Mexican history is remembered in their street signs; just pay attention to the names of streets, especially those that commemorate a date like Marzo 18, and you'll get an insight as to what's revered.

My favorite joke, which made the students laugh at revealed truth, was to pick on San Miguel de Allende, in my view the haven for

315

many pretentious expat American artists. When students asked if I liked Mexico, I mentioned places and events I enjoyed and expanded on my visits to Guanajuato and compared that city to San Miguel. I asked the students, "What is Guanajuato famous for?" Most students agreed, "momias (mummies)," macabre displays of disinterred corpses. They often failed to mention "Cervantino," which they regard as an opportunity for a student party like Fort Lauderdale's Spring break.

The mummies answer was the straight line I needed. I mentioned my experience in walking around, sightseeing in San Miguel, and the elderly American women who singly roam the streets and are so visible by their height, their large hats, billowy touristy Mexican attire, and artistic airs. The kids got it. Some had been to San Miguel and smiled. I asked, "Am I telling the truth?"

In chorus, "Yes" they called out. So the others believed.

Then, I advanced my interpretation: "In Guanajuato, they have good taste and bury the mummies in tombs, but in San Miguel, they allow them to walk the streets." The laughter woke up the sleepy ones.

In spite of limited time, or demanding school schedule, I attended the theater and a number of events. "*Con Amor a Mexico*," a marimba concert performed by students for free, was an absolute delight and was held in the ancient opera house. Later, I followed the Rondal, students dressed as 16th-century Spanish nobility in capes, puffy short pants, and long stockings, playing guitars and singing romantic songs, either love songs or sometimes risqué versions with double meanings, through the streets and into the university. I attended a cabaret, also Lorca's play "*La Casa de la Señora Bernada Alba*," saw "*Don Juan Tenorio*," and for the first time in a decade the opera "*Carmen*" performed by the Mexico City Company. And there were endless dances, bands, art shows and exhibitions, even puppet shows, in the six nearby plazas.

Mexican youth, particularly university students, venerate fabled pre-Columbian Indian culture and promote pre-Hispanic rituals.

Spain put a Catholic patina on pagan rites and now a student-led pagan revival adds a second decorative leaf. It appears that D.H. Lawrence's "The Plumed Serpent," written in 1926, foretold a present spiritual trend.

Students told me that kleptomaniacs rule the country, and corruption is accepted as inevitable. My barometer, taxi drivers, (less corrupt in the north than the south, whose meters never work, or are nonexistent) I test from time to time and pay the price. If you ask the price of the fare before you get in the cab you're likely to be quoted the official rate, the best price. When you ask, "How much do I owe?" at the destination, the likely answer is an inflated tab. In asking, you indicate to the driver that you are not familiar with the set rates, and his integrity quickly slides to a profitable answer.

Maybe Mexicans take first prize in shoeshines! Both my black walking shoes and black running shoes radiated a brilliant glow that made me watch my own feet glide over cobblestones with a pleasure only surpassed by a fresh can of Almond Royal chocolates. When sneakers took over the walking world, we lost the simple, profound pleasure of a glistening foot "feetish." Mexican "angelitos negros," must shine the black holes in space.

"University" loses something in translation. This university often is a two-year work-study program of 30 percent on the job, 70 percent in the classroom, based on the French model. Courses are practical, industrial, business and English, no liberal arts. I should not criticize any education; this is progress.

The students were friendly, courteous, frequently studied and worked under less than ideal conditions, and were making progress in English. It's a start. In fact, what I did notice was that many Mexicans now have some English at their command. Just a few years ago, when I traveled to Zacatecas, or when I made a seven-city bus exploration, English was not in evidence as I find it today. The best students invariably had lived in the U.S.

Queretaro continues to impress me in contrast to my visit in the early 1980s. Someone took charge, preserved the colonial center and created a cultural climate. There is also the ultramodern auditorium where I saw "*Carmen*," and where the handcrafts fair was held.

We finished our Queretaro assignment on a Friday with a mini-fiesta. I took charge of the entertainment. There was a long discussion among the group about what to bring to the party. Cheese, fruit and milk headed the list. So I said, "We're getting into too much work and creating a logistical problem." (The volunteers were decent, compassionate, caring, Mother Teresa types, but hadn't a clue about throwing an appreciation, good-bye fiesta for the Mexicans.) "I'll take care of it," I said.

Not far from the hotel was a first-class bakery named Edel Weiss, with a solid array of pastry delights. I bought a millewafer chocolate cake, a second chocolate cake with huge glazed strawberries, and custard cups crowned with glazed fruit. When I'm in charge, I buy what I like.

Then I searched for champagne. After discovering that wine and spirits were just not readily at hand, I told a taxi driver to take me wherever I needed to go to find champagne. Then, in honor of the great Mexican composer Juventino Rosa, I wrote new lyrics to "*Sobre las Olas,*" which we know as "*When You Are in Love,*" was emcee for the affair, and crooned:

We came to teach English,
Here in this beautiful place,
Now we must leave you,
We carry a very sad face.

Our hearts will return,
With many a memory,
Of wonderful students,
Teachers and faculty!

It was a success in spite of my froggy voice.

318

Mexico's divided class-cultures still catch me off guard. I hailed a taxi for the local WalMart for party napkins, plates and cups. Inside WalMart you're back in the USA, with the store surrounded by an enormous parking lot. The First Culture shops here.

I walked to the Mercado Escobedo, equally large, no parking, zillions of stalls, fresh fruit and vegetables, meat hanging, clothes, hardware, anything, if you can figure out which aisle to take and duck through. The Second Culture shops here.

My concern is that we are becoming Mexican faster than they are becoming us. The growing division between rich versus poor, tech-skilled versus menial labor, haves versus have nots, private school versus public is not the development I favor. Good jobs and near-tuition-free education invited me to California in 1958, but that Education Master Plan is now history. It's most apparent in hotel, restaurant, car wash, landscape gardening, and construction businesses that the owners are likely white, the workers brown. I prefer a bell-shaped culture, with the vast majority within one standard deviation versus the bimodal distribution model.

Mexico enjoys the good fortune that the Second Culture has a passive nature, responds to authority, feels fatalistic and doesn't terrorize the First, yet. Chiapas is on the verge.

The more I walked Queretaro's colonial center, which was about a half-mile square, if not larger, the more I realized that I had found a patio paradise. I couldn't determine if all these buildings were once convents, church related or private homes now converted. I peeped into the archways as I walked. Single-arched doorways opened into a patio with a fountain, sometimes working, but always beautiful and always raising the question, "What was the source of the wealth that built Queretaro's historic center, and who lived here?" Most of the buildings were shops, restaurants, and hotels, living a modern life in colonial garb.

I took my last comprehensive postcard mailing to the post office, sent all my former clients greetings and affixed each card with a bright, colorful stamp, just to let them know that I'm well, healthy and teaching in Mexico. I felt that one more postcard was in order so old clients would know that it wasn't just a business relationship, but that there was also a personal connection.

When our tour of duty ended in Queretaro, I was fortunate that three of our group wished to see more of Mexico. We visited the parents of a good friend, a restaurant owner from the hometown of two of the group. The parents lived in Sierra Gorda Mountains. They had eight children, none educated beyond junior high, and they lived in the high desert where you'd swear starvation ruled.

From his cinderblock house, which was as clean and shiny as my shoes, the 67-year-old father, raised chickens, goats, cows, grew vegetables, including corn that he dried and ground for tortillas, and nearly fifteen varieties of fruits, including a sour orange, with a tortured skin that I was unfamiliar with, which was used for cooking. From the road, you would never guess the productivity of that arid, hillside property.

We spent two days driving, twisting through the mountains, and visiting the Sierra Gorda range, the Franciscan missions and the churches. We stayed at a former hacienda. People rave about Sedona, its beauty and variety of vegetation, but I'm convinced that the Sierra Gorda takes the prized Blue Ribbon on both counts, and the missions, with unique façades mixing native and Catholic symbols, are added for good measure.

I made a quick run to San Luis Potosí, delivered a cake to a friend who guided my first trips to Mexico, dined with her and family then raced back to Las Campanas (The Bells), my hotel in Dolores Hidalgo, for the next Global Volunteer stint.

I stepped into my hotel room where the temperature had dropped below refrigeration. The climate in Dolores Hidalgo was mild, somewhat colder that normal, but I managed to find the coldest spot and a heat-sucking mattress. With two additional blankets, one to sleep under and the other to insulate me from the mattress, and with a nighttime get-up that only Eskimos would consider, I managed not to freeze. I slept with socks and slippers, with only moonlight and a light bulb for radiant heat. The moon wasn't full and the bulb flickered.

Subsequently, I learned how aptly named was my hotel, Las Campanas. The morning tintinnabulation of the bells, bells, bells, every ding and every dong, hundreds of them began at 5:30 a.m.

Dolores Hidalgo was real Mexico. When I inquired from the U.S. about parking for my car, I was told, "Oh, yes there is parking," but he failed to mention it was on the street. I found parking lot three blocks from the hotel where the "vigilancia" (security) locked the gate according to his personal schedule, so the Grand Marquis was secure, especially from me.

The new group of Global Volunteers jumped in average age by about ten years compared to the last group. All were experienced travelers, and the majority were either teachers by profession or had taken the English-as-a-second-language course. The core of our group, The Seven Sisters of Feminism, took none of my opinions. Our leader was pathologically cheerful, optimistic, loved everyone nonjudgmentally and believed in "sharing," which is one of my favorite gag-me-with–a-spoon clichés. Her good nature and friendships were the assets that got us invited to a ranchito barbecue where the sons of the hotel owner acted as chef and dance instructor. She deserved credit for an "all-come-over" house party invitation. We brought tequila and beer, and I surprised the group with the arrival of a mariachi band. Animal House would have been proud. And to my great delight, there was an arranged visit to the fabulous La California Hacienda built by Casimiro Peña, the Chili Pepper King of Mexico.

Rosalia Peña took us through her parent's hacienda, a mini-Hearst Castle, crammed with art and antiques, which her father purchased on his many world-travel trips. His well-executed plan was to bring back a little bit of each part of the world. At the end of the visit, I was left pondering, "How many chili peppers must a Mexican pick if a Mexican must pick peppers?" Zillion and zillions...

Without our leader, the town of Dolores Hidalgo could have been boring. Although it is the cradle of Mexican independence, an historic city with a museum and murals that honor its history, Dolores Hidalgo can be fully explored in forty-five minutes. Well, that's hyperbole, but not too much off the mark. It depends on how enchanted one is inspecting Talavera pottery, the economic staple of the town, and making a visit to the cemetery to see the glorious mosaic tomb dedicated to the singer José Alfredo Jimenez. Weekend side trips to San Miguel and Guanajuato were important if one wasn't to go stir crazy.

At the university, close to brand new, they required picture IDs so they scheduled a photo session with no film. Three hours later the film arrived, and we all lined up for our security pictures. But never were they requested, so I just kept mine warm in my wallet.

The class schedule in Dolores was as different from Queretaro as the town itself. We were expected to teach a maximum twenty hours per week, which made it a four-day week. Ironically, in the town with little to see or do, we had the greatest amount of free time. We taught mornings and some evenings.

We spent a day in a tiny, impoverished town, La Victoria, about an hour's ride away.

I took a second dose of Dr. Everett's Dumb Pills and made a side trip to Mineral de Pozos, a mining ghost town that reminded me of Real de Catorce without the exotic location. I soon found myself rappelling down a sixty-to-seventy-degree incline on the way to the bottom of an abandoned gold-silver mine 600 feet below the surface. Mexico's liability law is: "Keep your eyes open." Out of breath, in the black abyss, my guide pitched a stone into the mine's pure pool of water to show me that we'd reached the bottom. My female guide made an emphatic statement about any so-called superiority between the sexes. There was no question about who was the superior. I gave her the $5 fee plus $2 "for not leaving me at the bottom of the hole."

322

Then I drove to Xichu, which is isolated in the Sierra Gorda Mountains. I didn't find the end of the rainbow but I came close to the end of the earth. The last fifteen miles took me over a dirt road, through one-way tunnels, and the three crosses at the side of the road over looking the steep, one-mistake-and-it's-all-over chasm below, gave me no comfort.

After that adventure, I decided to keep it reasonable, so I enjoyed a hot springs, an Olympic-sized pool (four laps nearly killed me at the high altitude), and got a Mexican tan for my sunbathing effort.

■■

Recommended Books

I have my favorite books and authors to recommend. And if you understand Spanish, I suggest reading the lyrics of Mexican *corridos* and *mariachi* songs. A lot of history is in those songs, they're oral newspapers of their times. Translate *23 de Febrero* and you'll learn about Pancho Villa and the Mexican viewpoint. And if you read *La Cucaracha,* the lyrics may surprise you.

B. Traven, best known for *Treasure of the Sierra Madre*, is my favorite author. Of his books, I recommend: *Government*, (Don't be put off by the title.), *White Rose, Kidnapped Saint,* and *Night Visitor.* These stories capture the essence of the Indian-Mexican spirit. They are as true today as when Traven wrote them in the 1920s. Other books about Mexico by B. Traven include: *The Carreta, Cotton Pickers, General from the Jungle, March to the Monteria, Marcario, Rebellion of the Hanged,* and *Trozas.*

Many of these may be purchased used: try abe.com and Amazon.com.

History

An eyewitness account of the Spanish conquest: *The Discovery and Conquest of Mexico,* by Bernal Diaz Del Castillo. He's the Marco Polo of New World history.

323

The Conquest of Mexico by William Prescott: This is the classic. James Michener would call Prescott, "The source."

Cortes and the Downfall of the Aztec Empire by Jon White: Cultures collide.

Thomas Gage's Travels in the New World by J. Eric S. Thompson (editor). This is the only firsthand account of early Mexico by an Englishman. Thomas Gage, a Dominican friar, recounts his life and adventures in Mexico from 1625 to 1637. Particularly valuable for readers interested in Oaxaca, *Indian Mexico*, the church and its missions. At times, it reads like a spy novel.

Baron Alexander von Humboldt, *Political Essay on Kingdom of New Spain.* With a letter of introduction from the King of Spain, a scientist travels across Mexico in 1803. He records his travels and discoveries. He gives his views, illuminating and tabulating everything Mexican: plants, animals, geography, geology, and language. Supremely informative. Try to find a used, abridged copy.

Frances Calderón de la Barca, *Life in Mexico.* This Scottish lady, married to the Spanish Ambassador, keeps a diary (1839-1842) and writes lucid, humorous letters filled with observations about manners, people and events. Sometimes you think she is Balzac writing a novel.

Dane Chandos, *Village in the Sun* and *House in the Sun.* These two books were written in the early 1940s about the personal experiences of an expatriate who settled in Ajijic on the shore of Lake Chapala and became an innkeeper. It recounts the stories of the people he keeps and who keep him. The book is in English, but Chandos adds flavor, humor and understanding with dialogue literally translated. This is bittersweet for those who now visit Lake Chapala.

History: The Indians' Point of View

The Broken Spears: The Aztec Account of the Conquest of Mexico, by Miguel Leon-Portillo. The book relies on historical Aztec recollections.

Mexican Codices by Maria Sten provides clues to the pre-Columbian world.

Reading the Maya Glyphs by Michael D. Coe and Mark Van Stone is clearly written, easy to understand, an artistic pleasure and hard to absorb. First read is for pleasure, and then it's a must study.

The Mexican Dream, Or, the Interrupted Thought of Amerindian Civilizations, by J M G Le Clezio. The book presents a deep view of the personalities of the conquerors and the conquered, of Nezahualcoyotl, a poet, politician and despot, and speculations on what might have been.

Popol Vuh: The Mayan Book of the Dawn of Life, by Dennis Tedlock depicts the creation of the world. It's the Mayan bible.

History: The 1910-1920 Revolution

Barbarous Mexico: 1910 by John Kenneth Turner (no relation to Timothy Turner) begins with an interview of jailed Mexican revolutionaries in Los Angeles prison. Disbeliving their stories about the corrupt conditions in Mexico, Turner, with his friend Lazaro Gutierrez de Lara, goes undercover as an American investor and travels throughout Mexico visiting plantations and hacenderos. He goes behind Porfirio Diaz's Potemkin façade of progress and brings back the wretched reality of Mexico under Diaz.

Bullets, Bottles and Gardenias by Timothy Turner: A news reporter travels with Madero, Villa, Carranza, Obregon and reports on the Revolution. It's the best adventure book I've read in a decade. His descriptions are better than a camera. And he captures the personalities of the principals. This difficult-to-find book is well worth the effort and expense.

Diaz: Master of Mexico by James Creelman answers John Kenneth Turner and writes a favorable account of Porfirio Diaz, his youth, education, military experience and rise to power. It's an incredible story of the Iron Ruler of Mexico. It shows Diaz's tact, foresight, energy, nerve and intelligence in action. It's the heads side of a coin that never wants to see the tails. Creelman answers the critics with convoluted, rationalized reasoning that would put a college freshman to shame. It's well worth reading.

Chasing Villa, The Last Campaign of the U.S. Calvary by Col. Frank Tomkins.

Zapata and the Mexican Revolution by John Womack. This is recommended and deemed the authoritative history by Mateo Zapata, Emiliano's son.

Mexico: Biography of Power: A History of Modern Mexico, 1810-1996 by Enrique Krauze: A very readable, chronology of Mexico's leaders and their grasp and flow of power.

Social Studies and Opinions

Children of Sanchez by Oscar Lewis is a classic study of Mexican life.

Buried Mirror: Reflections on Spain & the New World by Carlos Fuentes is about cultures in conflict, rooted in the past, continued in the present.

Labyrinth of Solitude by Octavio Paz offers nine essays that examine the blended Mexican identity and consequences.
Bordering on Chaos: Mexico's Roller-Coaster Journey Toward Prosperity by Andres Oppenheimer offers insight into the political and economic turmoil of the 1990s.

Coyotes: A Journey Through the Secret World of America's Illegal Aliens by Ted Conover. The author spends a year immersed in the migrants' life and writes an insider's view of their hardships, joys and motivations.

God's Middle Finger by Richard Grant is an Englishman's journey into the lawless world of the Copper Canyon. Grant incorporates history with extreme current adventures. In his visit to the Copper Canyon, not taking the tourist route but driving an old truck past forgotten mining claims on roads that seem more suited for goats, Grant writes that it's the only place where picking up a hitchhiker increases one's safety, as bandits are more likely to attack a lone driver.

History in Novel Form

Mexico by James Michener is a formulaic novel that covers generations and educates the reader.

Power and the Glory by Graham Greene is the novel based on Green's journalistic report, which covered the anticlerical period of the 1920s, published as *Lawless Roads.*

Colonial Church Architecture

Blue Lakes and Silver Cities by Richard D. Perry covers west Mexico, 16th-century missions and murals. This is a highly illustrated text, and once you read the text and see Perry's drawings of the Sierra Norte Missions, you're likely to make it a destination.

City, Temple, Stage: Eschatological Architecture and Liturgical Theatrics in New Spain by Jaime Lara.

Movies with a touch of Mexico

Many films, once impossible to get, are now available on video and DVD. Facets Multi-media (www.facets.org) in Chicago is an important source for rental or purchase of the classics. But many may be bought on the Internet, especially used videos. Google is a good place to start, but you'll likely end up at Amazon.

Here's a list of Mexican movies (a very broad definition) that I've enjoyed. I chose them for: 1) pure entertainment, 2) setting, and 3) films with educational value: historical and cultural. My favorites:

History-Biography

Captain From Castile, Caesar Romero dons his helmet as Cortez and leads his Spanish troops in this conquest-adventure, which retraces the route of Cortez from Veracruz to Mexico City.

Juarez, stars Paul Muni and Bette Davis, a Warner Brothers Biography.

Reed: Insurgent Mexico is a dramatization of the 1910 Revolution that seems like a newsreel.

Viva Villa with Wallace Berry, Leo Carrillo and Fay Wray.

Viva Zapata stars Marlon Brando and Anthony Quinn, screenplay by John Steinbeck.

Some classics

Que Viva Mexico by Eisenstein, Sergei

Los Olvidados by Buñuel, Luis

Forgotten Village is a semidocumentary by John Steinbeck

Marcario, written by B. Traven, is in black and white. In this Mexican fable Traven shows more insight and compassion than an anthropologist.

The Pearl is John Steinbeck's 1947 fable of hope and despair filmed in the Sea of Cortez.

Great entertainment

I think we can all agree on *Treasure of Sierra Madre* with Humphrey Bogart, a tale of greed, with the unforgettable Alfonso Bedoya as the man in the Gold Hat.

Night of the Iguana with Richard Burton put Puerto Vallarta on the tourist map.

El Norte starts in Guatemala and winds up in California. Our heroes travel the length of Mexico. Insightful, comic-tragedy.

Touch of Evil has Charlton Heston playing a Mexican detective. Marlene Dietrich and Zsa Zsa Gabor have cameos, and Orson Welles plays the villain, right out of Shakespeare!

For the scenes shot at Las Hadas in Manzanillo, *10* with Bo Derek. And take a look at *Fun in Acapulco* with Elvis Presley.

Viva Max A Mexican brigade retakes the Alamo, a comic satire with Peter Ustinov. Pure joy. The sound track alone gets my vote.

Shot on location, John Huston captures a Mexican cultural kaleidoscope mixed with a diabolical explosion in *Under the Volcano.* The story follows three living, tortured souls on the Day of the Dead. Mature audience.

A tale of switched guitar cases, *El Mariachi,* gives us a gangland comedy of errors.

El Gringo Ambrose Bierce, a man of caustic wit, disappears and a new legend is born.
Tres Caballeros is Walt Disney's quirky homage to South of the Border.

Lady from Shanghai casts Rita Hayward as the center of attraction when the yacht docks in Acapulco before sailing north, tying up in San Francisco Bay and letting the bad guys shoot it out in the Fun House. It's a cinematic jewel.

La Rosa Blanca Written in the 1920s, this B. Traven story of oil exploitation in conflict with reverence for the land is modern in its environmental concerns.

Laurel and Hardy's, *The Bullfighters* is silly fun for the younger crowd. Laurel is misidentified as a matador.

Jaime Olmos stars in *The Ballad of Gregorio Cortez.* Cultural conflict creates suspicion, and misunderstanding brings tragedy. The story is told using two points of view, Rashomon style.

I'm sure I've missed a lot and I'd be glad to add to my collection. If you can suggest any, please do and include a short reason why you liked the film. Email me at: dickdavis40@hotmail.com.

Afterword

I wanted a lot of pictures to accompany each chapter of *Bus Journey Across Mexico.* The reader could see the complexity that is Mexico, the beauty, the variety, people and places, and because my descriptions were simply inadequate to the task. Besides, travelers could use some pictures for directions by opening the book, turning to a chapter, pointing to a photo, showing it to a taxi driver or someone on the street, and saying, "Here. I want to go, here." In my view, finger pointing is better than a GPS.

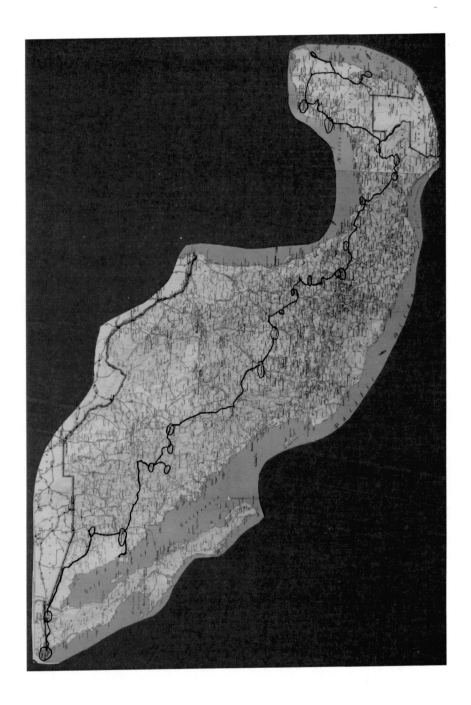

Bus Journey across Mexico